OUT TO SEE

Thank you for reading a book.

You're already helping.

OUT TO SEE

Jacob G. Roloff

Special thanks in editing to Isabel Rock (de Garretón)
and Jack Morrissey.

Cover art by Izzy Rock.

Second Edition; featuring corrections and additions to the text;
new cover art by Izzy Rock.

Published by Rock & Roloff LLC

ISBN: 978-1-7323312-0-4

RockandRoloff.com

For Toni and because of her love,
for giving the world Izzy, Nico and Toe

A family full of magic
always eager to share

It's safe to say
I wouldn't be here on these pages
without those four

These acknowledgments wouldn't be complete
without one to Lieutenant! Tomás, Sr. —

"when you're good, you're good!"

Contents

Preface

Having titled this book *Out To See*, I am at once acutely aware that I have much more to experience and learn, and also completely sure that I have left one place and arrived at another; left one stage of perception and arrived at another. I often struggle with the tone that I may carry in writing. However, there's an old Zen saying from Master Ummon where he says, "If you walk, just walk. If you sit, just sit, but above all, don't wobble." I try to remind myself of this all the time in order to get any writing done whatsoever.

I am tempted here to overcompensate with self-corrections, trying to present everything the perfect way with the perfect words, and perfect tone, but that effort would, I believe, take away some level of what I mean to accomplish in the first place, which is spontaneous and genuine expression.

So, with Master Ummon's words in mind, I do not want to spend too much time here or within defending my stance or the obviousness of all the experiences still to be had in my life. Instead of wobbling, trying to satisfy all the angles to all the rationales of every reader, I will just write. And you, just read. From Lao-tzu's Tao Te Ching:

Express yourself completely,
then keep quiet.
Be like the forces of nature:
when it blows, there is only wind;
when it rains, there is only rain;
when the clouds pass, the sun shines through.

13

The inspiration for this particular project came from a song by the same title, written and performed by my fiancée Isabel's late brother Tomás Rafael Garretón.

Jacob G. Roloff
August 2017

"This above all: To thine own self be true."

poems

Striving and striding
on. And on hopes—
for a better tomorrow;
for ambitions;
for office.

Strove or strode
I find:
here only.

Inescapable,
as it is,
ungraspable.

> To sing over the Classics
> to paint over the Romantics
> to eat for my health,
> and not for the taste;
> to work towards what is finished,
> the absurdity strikes me!
> O'
> To simply Be!

Continuing this life in stride,
scarcely towards trouble,
or causing myself strife—

I find myself
just walking.
Suzuki says floating,
"about two feet off the ground",
into and through
a perfect Today.

Brick, by brick

The dripping smile
The heaving
Of mans best friend.

Brick, by brick

Walking along,
A golden path from Oz,
Through early autumn leaves.

Brick, by brick

The flowing red hair,
Tangled,
Of my one lady love.

Brick, by brick

Gently falling snow
Atop a soft-lit town,
The likes you've only dreamed of.

Brick, by brick

Attending Christmas mass
in a language you don't know
with a little old woman
who can't help but
say hello . . .

Brick by brick,

Brick, by brick,

I'll paint you a picture of God

You're forgettable

You are forgettable,
like the purest in life.

The type of things
within:

Falling in love
and Falling out;
the absolute best, the worst
the joy, the pain;

the simple moments—
the complete experience—
the days that are all there
and,
all right;

the fragrance from
that candlelight.

You are forgettable,
"Like a pot of warm tea

You are easy to me…"

—a brief ode to Magister Ludi and the Game

Sometimes, I want nothing more than to read;
to clear my mind, to surrender to the vision
and the dream, of words written, and, now long gone.

"What could it be, that so prevents me?"

The tumult, distraction, and excess of our age
seem in part to blame.
The abundance in knowledge in wasteful excess:
of things, of happenings, and of times moved on,
put us in quite the peculiar and difficult position—
unique to our time.

The highest feat it seems now-a-days,
comes from our choices in negation:
"Of what will you abstain?"

I find it to be quite healthy—lo, the prerequisite to health
—abstaining from the scurry, the fury, the worry of our time,
by retreating into thy self and thine life.
Not of pure and selfish desire,
but of rapture in some irreplaceably prized leisure-time;
dazzling us, and our mind's eye.

Of *my* highest prize, there is no doubt:
the memory of a day disappearing in-to a good book,
as they once did when I was a kid.
Alas, the tide of time is relentless, and,
I have lost this ready capacity of sitting just so,
immersed in the words and the worlds that I read; complete.

Of late however, blessed by God,
I have had little trouble in reentering
this magic literary bubble.

Be it the words, the story, the meaning, the man,
or all altogether—I cannot resist any return visit that I can,
unplanned, to the land of Castalia:
the most welcome of phantasma.

Our primitivity is evident
when seen through the lens of this place, it seems;
for there we are known, as the feuilleton.

This phantasmic place, no doubt, and in no special haste,
renews in my immersion a long-lost child-mind of mine;
back to when I was able to forget my self,
and to chase a papillon simply, because.

Now, again.

All in thanks to these four hundred pages plus,
turning, turning on.

In our world of apparent void and point-less noise,
Castalia is, to make it abundantly clear:
A Welcome—
and Joyous
—Phantasm.

"Our God is <u>alive</u>. Sorry about yours!" Unknown

the three

a few brief points regarding Taoism, Hinduism, and Buddhism; their effect on my state of mind, and disposition towards the world.

In the last few years, I have become fascinated by some of the traditions and philosophies of the Far East. However, I find it difficult to convey what I mean, as surely these ways of thinking from the other side of the world are structured and evolved in a much different way than religions common throughout the West: Islam, Judaism, and Christianity, and thus can not be described using the same familiar words without some clarification. Representing the East, generally there are Buddhism, Taoism, and Hinduism, which are understood as being more philosophical and reflective—rather than dogmatic and strictly structured.

From the point of view of an average Western person—Judaism, Christianity, and Islam are, in the normal sense and structure, religions. They each have dogma, hierarchies, priests, and a God modeled after a kind of King, Lord of all creation, who all must serve, metaphorically or otherwise. There is a common image held with holy reverence "above" what we know as everyday existence. They are each distinctly a means for *salvation* from this earthly body with all of its temptations and sin.

Then there is Buddhism, Taoism, and Hinduism, which have in my experience been slandered and propagandized against as polytheistic—a superficial understanding that

"God is everything." And although they may contain such tendencies, they are wholly more than just one nugget of truth, so easily extracted.

We are born and raised with this Western idea of God and morality, and so naturally upon hearing of these far away mysteries we measure them against what we already hold as true. But how could we ever expect to understand such a foreign system, if we only study it under the lens of our own, which has developed half a world away. Moreover, a perspective that we are undeniably predisposed to.

This isn't to say that one could not keep whichever system he likes as a sort of compass through life—"let all those operate a ferry boat who will." It is only to say that learning about another is an exceptional pleasure and a genuine opportunity for growth. Learning about a different way of life is really meeting a completely different mind.

I feel, that to have a chance at truly experiencing such a different way of thought, and to meet another mind, one must temporarily *reserve,* completely and truly, the ideas that they carry from the religion given to them by their parents and culture.

Let us just say, put simply, that you've got a peanut butter and jelly sandwich. That's all you or anyone you know ever eats and it's gotten you along just fine. Then someone suggests to you that there may be a sandwich that tastes just as good if not better—tuna maybe. Would you resist trying the new thing because you fear the old thing just might never come back? Would you set down your peanut butter and jelly sandwich, take the two pieces of bread apart, and insert a Tuna sandwich in the middle to find out if you liked it? If so, besides deciding that you hated the taste, you'd make sure to thereafter assert the inferiority of tuna, without ever having given it its proper chance!

In my initial exploration into this sort of inner realm, I was fortunate enough for it to be borne from discontent; it was not difficult for me to set aside my inherited system to go off and be curious about others. Of course this isn't the only way, for you may be a true Christian or whatever else right now and still examine these Eastern mysteries sincerely.

There need first be some clarification on how you think faith operates, in practice. Faith in *theory* is instead what we call belief; in *practice*, it's letting go—giving up the fight—for you know everything is the will of God, the will of the Self, Brahma or the Tao. If you trust completely in the dogma and belief system of your religion, there should be no problem abandoning it for the moment to learn about another—that is, to have true faith. For clinging desperately to something is not faith at all but acute insecurity, mixed in with a prideful sense of failure at "letting go"—of giving in to the feminine principle of yielding, among other things.

The situation a lot of people may find themselves in can be compared to wearing color-hued glasses, being here Christianity or any other 'unseen' guide to the way one might think—unseen for it underlies their very vision. And these folks look out onto the world and view it in terms of that color, that thing, that system. The way to see clearly is to realize—"to make conscious what is unconscious"—that you are under a ruse in the first place, that there is something distorting your worldview, whereafter you may see the world more honestly with these 'glasses' removed. The choice would finally be yours—for the very first time. This letting go, this relinquishing, is indeed the truest act of faith, whereas many people who see themselves as "of the Faith" only *believe*; really hard, to their credit, and probably with the best of intentions. It's a subtle distinction however, and it could mean the world. Belief is what you say to convince yourself, and others, that maybe *one day* what you're saying will have basis—belief is betting. If a person were afraid of the dark, and they found themselves strolling along the sidewalk beside a looming forest, they might repeat reassurances, prayers, or verses of all sorts while trembling in fear. On the other hand, a person with a measure of inner certainty and with faith in the world *as-such*, might walk by the very same forest without anything in their mind but perhaps the wind rustling the pines, or the sound of a hooing owl. This person has the faith to let go of trying to control the outcome by knowing through analysis, of knowing all possible ways the experiencing could be experienced, and in turn begins to know life *directly*. They become present to each moment with all its beauty and horror. Looking out onto the world, you can choose to see it as either one, for "the world is love to him who treats it as such, even when it torments and destroys him."

Therefore one may ask, whatever religious or philosophical system one has been raised with, how should we learn to encounter another? By reciting passages for illusory protection? Or are we capable of observing and learning with genuine interest and wonder, continuing then on our way? ..taking, if nothing else, another experience..

I'm going away,
I'm going out to see

Stepping back to reflect on the influence these ideas of the East have had on me, I realize that ultimately all I have learned from them so far may be supplemental to a better understanding of Christianity. This is not to say that I would choose to wrangle my worldview into any one system of belief—I think that ship sailed long ago for my own sense of intuition and general disposition, pertaining to my inner life. However I now consider myself more of a Christian than ever before, while maintaining the capacity to consider myself as more of a Buddhist than ever before, or a Taoist. As Chuang-tzu said, "The ideal mind is like a mirror; it grasps nothing; it refuses nothing; it receives, but does not keep." Through this way of thinking about religion, they all become supplemental to a more ultimate, inclusive, and more immediate knowledge.

A mirror is just *with* everything it reflects, but it does not keep any one image with exclusivity. As Alan Watts pointed out in his 1951 book *Wisdom of Insecurity*: to hold on to a mental image of God from whichever religion or myth is just as idolatrous as any physical statue, for, "Nobody can confuse a wooden image with God, but you can very easily confuse a set of ideas with God..."

He mentions also a Zen story where on a particularly cold night in a monastery the Master walks up to a dwindling fire, grabs a wooden statue of the Buddha, and throws it into the flames for a little extra warmth. When one of the monks protest the disrespect, the Master replies, "I'm only trying to get at the Buddha-nature." The monk asks, "How could you expect to know the Buddha (the ultimate Reality) through a piece of wood?" To which the Master replies, "If it is only a piece of wood why do you chastise me for burning it?" The next morning the Master was found carving another statue in the Buddha likeness and praying before it.

This is to say, among other things, that there is folly in taking symbols too seriously, while, though, reverence still holds its place. It seems reminiscent of another well known Zen story:

> *A monk asks his master, "How do you practice Zen?"*
> *The master replies, "When you're hungry: eat, when you're tired: sleep."*

And in terms of the story of burning the statue, "When you're cold: more fuel for the fire, when you crave holy communion: worship." The Eternal Now, and knowing and utilizing its creative essence, is Zen—if one must describe it. "Explaining" Zen is regarded by Buddhists as putting legs on a snake—unnecessary, and even cumbersome. It is best conveyed by its massive canon of stories that neither explain nor prophesy, but point. "Just look, would you?"

As a society, we seem too focused on what has been or what's to come to properly care for what's right under our nose. The only (or the first and primary) reality is the appropriate response to Now, for if you are a thinking individual, you exist Now, and not in the memories of the past or ideas about the future. All ideas—including past, future, all you think you know of God—are ultimately mere ideas. Their weight is measured in the concrete reality of the body and organ of the brain, consciously pondering. This is to the same tune of, "Jesus did not need Christianity to be saved", for he had good works and a life lived through love—infinitely more important things than an empty formula towards the same outcome. Instead of talking about a body walking around doing good works, he moved his legs, lifted his arms, helped the poor and the sick, and eventually died for the ultimate good—sacrifice of self. A life lived through love *is* what Christianity preaches. It has only become empty-as-formula through platitudinous overuse—catchphrases and nothings, uttered only for completion of the steps, not actual knowing, and much less feeling. And this is key, for obviously the principles, actions, and words 'contained in' Christianity existed before some fellow came along and named this extraordinarily impactful collection: "Christianity". And so the fault lies not in what is called Christianity, but in its sham adherents—those who preach for image and self-security, not for truth and sacrifice.

But for all the exploring I have done and continue to do, I still won't be able to escape these terms in which I have been brought up to think about religion in its most basic and unnoticed ways. I used to resent that notion, but have since come to appreciate it as my *svadharma*. I have seen this word translated as "one's own vocation" or "our own current, unique manner of being." It means, essentially: life as experienced through what you feel as "I", now. And that 'now' is forever changing, of course; building on itself for the life of itself.

Context for this word is found in Hindu mythology, where we are all seen as the masks, the different *persona[1]*, of Shiva, the Great Actor.

Shiva plays the hero, the villain, the addicted, the selfless, the layman, the educated, the fool.., and She goes all

[1]   The Latin origin of person, used in its time to describe the megaphonic mask that actors would wear in amphitheater to amplify their voice.

in with the performance until forgetting herself as all the best actors do, going as far out as she can, to the extremes of each experience however beneficent and menacing it might come to be. The life of any of these particular masks has a very specific and necessary role, which would be its svadharma.

Embracing my svadharma means here simply: not denying what is. For I don't need to pretend that I have the linguistic, cultural background of any other religion, that I'm some 'other' role. I can say that God is love, and He lives, without succumbing to spiritual pride in the fact that "someone will misunderstand me." That point is already unavoidable. Additionally, the avenues that one can go down by description are infinite; you can never fully wrangle the needlepoint of an instant—a fleeting moment where a thousand and one things are interacting with their thousand and one counterparts—birds, bees, blood cells, you and me—all of existence!

Incidentally, I think another meaning to svadharma I rather enjoy is "return to origin," as if to center oneself by a realignment of your internal, intellectual compass. For if not for this process and realignment, one might try to let on that they're a Buddhist, loudly searching for enlightenment, and trying to turn others toward that path, but that would be phony, and a pretending. Therefore, my origin is as a Western man, born into a Christian family. I will never be able to struggle free from the subtleties of that heritage, and that is perfectly fine. As you'll see, this is more freeing than it is constricting, for I am able then to forego the wasting of energy fighting simply what *is*.

After knowing this, it opens the door to seeing clearly and sincerely other points of view. This is not to say that a person cannot change, or that one's life is predetermined, neither that you exist in a nebulous state with no feeling or attachment. Many people, I have found, see this to be a summation of Eastern philosophy. However that is a grave misrepresentation. This seeming paradox of determination and free will is where two other words have come to mean a lot to me: *judo* and *bodhisattva*.

Judo is probably the more familiar of the two, and means "gentle way" or "way of least resistance". Judo could be understood as the opposite of svadharma, which denotes such a determined idea, but it also goes with it in a special way by allowing a certain and necessary margin of interference *in* the determined. Only, however, if energy is applied *at the proper moment*, which is the principle for attack in the judo martial art. This moment, as well as the judo applied, become in that instant part of the same process as your vocation and calling, and are not then interferences but *intertwined and one with* what always was supposed to be; what simply *is*.

Then, bodhisattva—a Buddhist term for "a person whose essence is perfect knowledge." Also in other sects of Buddhism, like Mahayana, bodhisattva refers specifically to an enlightened one who has chosen to *remain* within the circle of life and death (*samsara*) in order to help others and to be an example to the world from which he came, and belongs.

Relating that official definition to my own life, I find it doesn't fit particularly well. However, I have redefined it and applied it just the same. Rather than the existential titles of samsara and enlightenment, I could say I have simply been unplugged from a rose-hued haze of belief. It carries more of a personal meaning where you might say that I have abandoned my origin religion—my svadharma—to seek more, and to learn all I can. Now, at the least, I understand that there is no conflict between where I come from and where I'm going in regards to these beliefs, so abstract in their nature. They build on one another forever, or rather, keep flowing and chasing each other forever. There is no need for me to renounce what came before, because it has ultimately, in whichever way you see it, brought me to this point of freedom where I can pronounce my love of God, but without feeling the shame of regression; for it is all at once, the culmination of what has been manifests what is now, so where am I regressing?

In sum, this whole project, and writing publicly as a whole, could be seen to be my 'bodhisattvaic' attempt to let people, anyone, coming from a similar Western religious background know that these philosophical mysteries of the East—the Three—contain an abundance of wisdom. And in fact we *can* learn a great deal from them. For I have been in the position of contemplating the other side of the spectrum in atheism, and abandoning, running away from reality. I want to let people who are in similar situations see my own personal doubts, as they are, as I write, and feel all-right about their own. There is a lot to love and appreciate in this world, and as you tread water in such a vast expanse of different ideas, it might help to be reminded of the company you share.

I've left this world behind
I'm going out to see

After coming to understand the relativity of religious language, it's hard to think of them the same way again. And I certainly don't mean relativity in a way that lessens the value and doesn't acknowledge the impact of each respective religion and their native language. I only mean that there are, in fact, other ways in which the world is seen, and so described. Religion is simply the symbolism we impose on forces higher than ourselves in an effort to understand, even rudimentarily grasp, what the world is making us feel—as long as we're paying attention. Seen as such, it can be described in as many ways as there are minds. In this realization of relativity, it seems I have left one place of perception, thoroughly focused on symbols of all sorts, and arrived at another that is—"of itself, so" (自然)—including the world of symbols, but not so uncontrollably fascinated by them.

A simpler way to approach this may be through dialogue, and answering some of the most prudent questions in my readers' minds. I will phrase these as if you the reader is asking them, as I'm sure many might be.

———

"So you believe in God, then?"

Absolutely. However, I should first ask what saying so means to you? To answer the question with any clarity, I would have to start by describing my individual perception of what actually saying 'God' means, and measure it against your own. It is easy to agree that the noise "chair" means: because we can picture a similar form of it in our head; *defined*. With such an ambiguous and misunderstood word such as God, it's more than "yes" or "no", "this" or "that".

So I'll get right into this as best I can.

The fundamental thing I believe to be true about God, though, is essential non-duality—one of those terms you can talk in circles about, which may indeed be part of the point. You cannot *get at* the non-duality of God, that is to possess Him in a description. You also can't claim to know what a non-dual God *stands* for, possessing Him morally or spiritually, while claiming also to have faith in that God—for that isn't trusting the unknown in Him at all. Its precisely the opposite: creating, or adopting, an image of what *you* think is suitable and reasonable, and having 'faith' that this scenario of your own creation is waiting for you at the end. You may have bought someone's idea, or created your own rendition, which is perfectly fine—but it simply is not faith, especially not of an insurmountable and omniscient God.

I believe in God to the extent that the word means, quite vaguely, Higher Thing We Cannot Describe, Who Yet Still Fills The World With Love and Creation and Destruction and Art and The Ten Thousand Things. I do not at this time care to idealize a God that has specific rules or a particular "look" or, most of all, a preferred people. If God does not reside in the base of *all* things, *all* people, what or who is it that stands apart, comparable, and equal to God? Furthermore, if God is in all things, then nothing is with*out* him.

If a person renounces all previously held ideas of God and feels this thing to be true—the Incarnation, which truly means God made flesh, God made Now, in the base of all things—he can appreciate once again the multitude of ideas and myths of God because they are each God's own way of knowing, seeing, hearing, and describing himself. Perhaps I should add here that packaged so to speak with the non-dual nature of God is His eternality. So to say that, "I believe in God," seems to me now a bit funny in that odd, 'putting legs on a snake' kind of way. As if one had a choice, as a thinking individual, who's just blinked themselves into existence, in having a God and Beginning, and a Higher Meaning.

But this is where another major misunderstanding happens. For people still, even if warned to suspend preconceptions, attach their institutionally-biased ideas to the word 'God'. Now, it may in fact be impossible to detach yourself from those unconscious views and ideas *completely*, but it isn't hopeless for understanding. For you can simply choose to listen and absorb *sincerely* another idea, even if it's way out there *when received in terms of your own idea.*

The only thing stopping a person from an understanding of this sort would be fear that this mysterious darkness one is encountering might flood one's mind and take over—as everything unknown is presupposed as sinister. As John Taylor Gatto says about education, "People would rather go with a system they *know* will fail, as opposed to adopting a new system that *might* fail." Meaning here that people would rather, for the sake of security and continuity, double down on their same-old way of seeing things, refusing to 'rock the boat.'

It seems to me that we are misusing this idea of religion. We are supposing that religion is the purpose and the end of our spiritual life. To what end is the perfection of prayer and meditation, the memorization of verse and sutra, and the attendance to church service? We act as if it's salvation or realization or something else, but as an old Buddhist simile says it, that is only "to look at the finger pointing the way, and then to suck it for comfort, rather than follow [it to that which it points]."

The Three

Our conception of symbols relating to reality is all jumbled in such a way that we "suck" the symbols hoping to attain reality. We solidify and put on a pedestal this way of describing the world in religion, in such a way that does not befit its nature, nor its potential. Religion in all its varying form is a finger pointing and not at all *final* in its purpose.

We speak different languages all around the world, and don't realize that the same is true of a sort of religious language, or metaphysical language. You find parallels still, though, in so many of these traditions. This is the "One without a second" expressing itself in all forms and ideas, for each person and culture. Each system is important *because* not everyone speaks the same language, so one idea you think is ridiculous or even unintelligible might invoke deep, lasting meaning in someone else by resonating with their own specific cultural background. There is no scale or measurement for predicting exactly which ideas will touch which people. Each set of ideas needs rather to be respected and allowed in its own right—wholesale—open to connection and also misuse by whomever. To be comfortable with that requires first to trust in the natural way of things, the Tao and God in the most inclusive sense. There is no one formula to define reality, and you cannot simply ban what you misunderstand, or avoid the uncomfortable. And religion, being itself a symbol, is conveyed as well by symbolic language, and thus should not be taken too seriously, in the sort of way that we mean when asking, "Is it serious?", about a deep gash or twisted ankle. By understanding religion in this very different way and not seeing it as *definitely* final, it becomes possible to give up the fight. You can begin to dive in to another way of thinking without fear or shame of abandonment, because, well… its just not that type of serious!

If you say God is loving, good, and graceful, then you also implicitly mean God is hateful, malicious, and rough. If it were not so, then that negative principle would stand apart from the positive as a contender, at which point there would be One, and Another "Higher Things"—God and the Devil equal on the scales. But seeing that there is "this" and "that" one eventually wonders where *they* came from, and this line of questioning can continue forever. And furthermore, setting something as equal to God would not make Him Ultimate or God so much as 'ultimate' and 'god'. A god standing opposed to some other figure is not the First and Final Source, but rather a symptom of it. So if you allow the possibility of your God being specific to one side of morality or anything else, what would this mean for the beginning of this opposing side, and thus the universe?

This personification of evil in the Devil or Satan, I suppose, is taken too literally, as if he is really this other entity standing equal, different, and opposed. The Devil is more likely an analogy for the fact that a non-dual God can not be described as only good, for that would exclude evil (understood from our human and ego perspective, at least. For it is obvious that from a non dual point of view there need be no naming or distinction, and the so-called evils of man would be known to 'serve' the eternal Good of God—the Infinite Point of View). God's own evil principle had no way of being described without despairing that life is mere meaningless suffering. So it was, for better or worse, attributed instead through an analogy by way of Satan and so many other figures.

Negative and Positive, Yin and Yang, God and Devil, Good and Evil, these are the terms we, as humans in a dual world, are forced to use. At some point, though, language goes no further, and we are left forever asking, "Well, what created this one?" which isn't to say that nothing is 'there' preceding and above these Yins and Yangs of existence. The precedent is neither some 'other' separate thing above the two before it, but a *joining* of the two things that we *thought* were separate and opposing. The joining, the being of union, is where God resides. In Marriage, Harmony, Love, Connection, Community, Music. All these things, in their ten thousand forms, are ways of feeling and understanding this eternal and symbolic union. The two poles invoke the connection, and the connection invokes the two poles. As an aside, this God is in truth neither before nor above any other thing. This is where all those omni- words come into play; for if God was before or above, He would not be omnipresent and eternal. If God did not know both Good and Evil, He would not be omniscient, and so on.

You see, God is not any *thing in fact,* for He existed before thing was indeed distinct from thing. He simply is— like air—like an emptiness of the sort that contains it all. His nature cannot be grasped through words, just as you cannot breathe by saying, "breathe"—it just happens, and so it is with this Now. We assume there is 'I' who 'breathes', but transcending that dual relationship is the thing itself: breath. We think there is you or I but really there is just the Happening. That essence of immediate inescapability is the closest I can get to describing my God. His infinity is best represented, paradoxically, with the things of this temporal world. For we, as unified in our nature and not a separate I, cannot step out of this world to use infinite and eternal vocabulary or adopt its point of view. That would be like trying to solve a Rubik's Cube by force and not intellect. So using temporal, changing, and immediate life happenings are indeed the best way to point to a meaning that transcends our very comprehension, and thus needs to be said in such a roundabout and poetic way. You see this all the time in Zen Buddhist stories, and it is what earns Zen the slanderous name of polytheistic.

Zen understands that we, as the persona of Shiva or Brahma or the Tao, are bound to our role as humans living in a finite, dualistic world. We should, then, act our part wholeheartedly. Go all in with what you is, just as Shiva does with your very existence. For you as the persona are finite, and should thus use the right language to communicate, sparing such confusion as arises with the interpretation of holy books and their analogies for the definite and infinite.[2]

---

[2]   This is due, really, to the blurry line of understanding between historical facts and mythological meaning. Myth is often misunderstood as meaning sort of 'fake story,' with decidedly less power than a parable. As Joseph Campbell put it, "Myths are public dreams; dreams are private myths." Myth is not useless or blasphemous, but metaphorical of a more

The Three

One of my favorites of these Zen stories tells of a master who has to choose his successor for the monastery. He puts his students to a test by presenting them with what Zen calls a *koan* (koh-ahn), which is a question phrased as a sort of contradiction provoking a state of meditation, hopefully to the student's eventual enlightenment.

This master gathers his students and presents them with his koan. He places a pitcher of water on the steps and says, "Without making any affirmations or denials, what is this?" Several of the monks who thought themselves to be rather clever and top of the class went to the master with their answers, but each one was sent back to continue contemplation. Eventually, the cook happened by the scene and, seeing the koan written on some parchment, kicked the pitcher over, walked away, and the master named him the new head monk first thing in the morning. For if the students had found some clever way of describing it, what would that mean, really?

P-i-t-c-h-e-r?

Just fancy, intricate, symbolical noise for the real deal. The only way to give it reality is to interact with it—knock it over, pour the water, or do nothing at all. Any words in and of themselves that might have been used would not be the real thing, for words alone are symbols. Only combined with action or reflection do they take form. Furthermore, it's well worth analyzing what are you choosing to interact with in each moment before you, and what that interaction is bringing to fruition! *Pura vida.*

I will never be able to perceive religion or God the same way as before, after dabbling in these 'mysteries from the East,' and I have only scratched the surface! Although Christianity is where I come from, I have gone out to see

---

infinite truth, symbolized by the world we know or a Heaven or Hell or any other perceived higher realm, although they always contain the attributes of a human consciousness [emotion, time, purpose, etc.].

and I'll never be back alive as the same person. I imagine this situation as a sort of miner seeking understanding and connection on deeper levels to the people and nature around him—to God. And as he digs and digs and digs for these answers, he seems to cross a line in the middle point of highest intensity, and doubt, where everything seems to change. But there his same ol' body still is—how curious. It is as if he dug down so deeply into the Earth he crossed the equator, where gravity and magnetism all flip; but there he is digging along in the 'same direction' as the 'same person'. And just like that, at the exact moment of plunging into the unknown, past the moment of highest intensity—utter freedom. I have likewise broken out into a wide open sea of direct experience. And so suddenly! As if my whole life leading up to this mysterious moment was just necessary pressure building for the release— for reasons unbeknownst. Now, as the pressure builds again, who knows what I will learn and feel and experience. After all, when you dig so far *down* that you cross that invisible equator of struggle, everything is *up* from there.

"What about those Holy Books?"

I fear I have been speaking rather negatively on the subject of religion—which I mean in the sense of literal negation, of removing certain images and concepts. This is because, according to my own belief, God is so much more than any one of them—which is of course itself an idea. As an idea alone it might be called atheism or agnosticism depending where you are on the spectrum, but in concert with actual experience of union with God, you can praise Him through his suggested and self-evident existence in all things. Although you might gather, correctly, that images and symbols in idea or morality do not wholly express Him, He still presents Himself within them through such things as divine inspiration and analogy. Furthermore, I believe God is fundamentally immediate and self-evident. You don't need to think about anything, or nothing, nor praise Him nor remain silent in order to know him now. "He fills up the ponds as he empties the clouds / He holds without hands and He speaks without sounds."[3]

And although I speak of God by using Him, that is due solely to my foundation and familiarity with the Christian faith. He is obviously, after all I've said, no-He, no-She, no-One, no-Being, and so on. Theres a Hindu saying, *neti neti*, meaning "not this, not this." It is sometimes used when talking about God because, being infinite, He cannot be this or that finite thing.

A First Century monk by the assumed name of Dionysius the Areopagite was credited for popularizing a word for the same type of negative speech in regards to mysticism and God: apophatic. Thus far I have been suggesting a reconsideration and shedding of ideas—altogether ignoring the remaining value in such tools for realizing God as the Bible, Upanishads, or the Tao Te Ching, religion in general. These all create images of God or the nature of realization, and so use cataphatic, positive language.

To answer the question then, "What about the Holy Books…", I would say: "Let all those operate a ferryboat who will."

In other words, what *about* them? Let whomever needs them, use them. They are special and necessary in their own right, and in their own place, and most certainly of divine inspiration—as is all good art. They do not, however, need to be conflated as anything equal *to* God. Religions and their books are to God as landscape paintings are to a mountain range—analogous. Although being analogous, paintings still move people to tears, and these books still lead people, directly and indirectly, onto the road toward union and realization. They also have their obvious historicity. Miracles and the like are granted as well, for I think miracles happen all the time. Waking up every day. Your lungs continuing to filter air. The fact that I could be blind, but by a miracle—or if I was a pessimist I'd say dumb luck—tiny broken pieces of my skull

---

3   *The King Beetle On a Coconut Estate*, by mewithoutYou (2009)

just barely avoided my optic nerve in a childhood accident. And life itself, the tree in the backyard, is utterly miraculous.

"How wild it is, to be anything at all!"

I am personally inclined to say neti neti and speak apophatically about God and the nature of reality, nevertheless I appreciate greatly the existence and use of cataphatic language and tools. Although it exists all around me, I'm particularly fascinated by music which is introspective and revealing of larger truths. From Chance The Rapper's *How Great* to Kendrick Lamar's *GOD.* to Logic's *Hallelujah* to Kanye's *Ultralight Beam*, they each express God from their respective points of view, and it's fascinating and extraordinary all at once to watch these household names speaking to an American youth who are seeking desperately again for something to put their faith and energy in; something to "make the game worth the candle."

FROM CHANCE THE RAPPER'S *How Great*:

> *The first, is that God is better, than the world's best day. / God is better, than the best thing that the world has to offer. ...*
> *Magnify, magnify, lift it on high / The Book don't end with Malachi. / Devil will win employee of the month by the dozen, / 'til one score and three years from the third when he doesn't.*

The world's best day... not this. The best the world has to offer... not this. Then, turning cataphatic, the next lines are to remind us of the Incarnation in the New Testament, as indeed the Book does not end with Malachi, that God is risen in man forever through the Incarnation—a source of optimism and creativity so powerful that it drowns out and pacifies the many evils of the world. For "..the world is love to him who treats it as such, even when it torments and destroys him."[4]

This power through incarnation is often mistook as being a privilege reserved for Jesus of Nazareth alone, supposing he is the real son of God, making all other children of God mere pretenders, apparently. However Chance embodies that exact optimism and creativity in his work and thus (illumines) the realization of the infinite Incarnation, the omnipresence and omnipotence of God—in himself and all of you.[5]

From Kendrick Lamar's *GOD.*:

> *This what God feel like.. : Laughin' to the bank like, "ahhh, ha!"*

These lyrics, as all the others, can be read in whichever way you see fit. But for me, it very well may be seen to imply the transcendence of common morality in the nature of God—being of course "above" all things. And of course not literally above, or any other direction—not even inside!—as pantheism suggests, for that would exclude outside. Alas, in words we cannot wrangle His nature without doubling back to say, "But not that!" He is simply beyond—beyond especially—morality. He is the charitable as well as the murderous. And He is indeed "laughin' to the bank", a colloquial way of saying "to worry not." After all, what *would* God worry about?

For in the end, according to the Hindu myth, the Great Actor Shiva wakes up and realizes only herself, thus ending all the roles that she played, and the universe itself—only

---

[4]   *This Is It* by Alan Watts (1973)

[5]   This and all forthcoming interpretations are strictly symbolic, even mythological. Each artist has different meanings for each selection to be sure, and each listener has their own way of listening. However I have this in mind as I write, from Watts' *The Supreme Identity*: "The principal importance … lies in its mythological character, that is, in what it incarnates or projects of that spiritual and interior realm which lies below the level of ordinary consciousness."

to begin again æons after. God Himself has not one thing to worry about because He *is* all of the assuredness *and* worry in the world. In all things. And we are simply the roles He plays for the gratuitous and simple pleasure of surprise, of going far, far out into each role. So what, in an existential sort of way, do we have to worry about—these persona, living and dying, rising and falling, as naturally and unwaveringly as ocean waves. . .

FROM LOGIC'S *Hallelujah*:

> *I'm like, Hallelujah! Praise God. Almighty, the Most High. Alpha and Omega in the sky...*
> *Made in the image of God, with a blunt in my mouth an' a bitch on the side...*

Logic has clearly gained perspective on what religion means to him, and its symbolical nature as a whole. He likely grew up with Christianity being the primary religion in his life—even if it wasn't actively practiced, we are all in the United States living in a Christian society—and just as likely, abandoned or did not fully adopt it as it was presented to him. Still, though, he is able to use such familiar praises for God as Almighty. Alpha and Omega. Then he says the seemingly contradictory thing of being made in His image with a blunt in his mouth and a bitch at his side—as if all men were truly allowed to operate as they will, under God.

I personally don't care for using this word to describe women, but I suspect he did so for an ulterior purpose in symbolism. The entire theme of the album is inclusion "for every race, religion, color, creed, and sexual orientation" leading me to believe he is likely implying something to the effect of God's image not being confined to any one creed of morality. Any so-called desirable behavior is subject to the time and place *of* that behavior, and thus cannot be a description for the Infinite. Logic is questioning what we think we know about such morals. As if to ask, "What qualifies *you* to judge anyone?" This is in line with *Matthew 7:1-4,* where Jesus says, "Pass no judgment, and you will not be judged. For as you judge others, so you will yourselves be judged, and whatever measure you deal out to others will be dealt back to you. Why do you look at the speck of sawdust in your brother's eye, with never a thought for the great plank in your own?"[6]

"Bitch at the side"? "Blunt"... drugs? Logic wants you, if for nothing else, to bring your prejudice and moral pride to the forefront of your consciousness. Look at it!

His album as a whole does an expert job at that. In this, his God is represented in all races, religions, colors, creeds, and sexual orientations—and so remains infinite.

AND... FROM KANYE'S *Ultralight Beam*:

> *This is a God dream. This is a God dream, this is a God dream. We on a Ultralight Beam, we on a Ultralight Beam! This is a God dream, this is everything.*

This verse conjures in my mind a certain sense of surrender. Surrendering to the notion that there are things higher than man. Things we may never be able to even grasp. As I listen to these words, I remember my recent visit to Yosemite, a beautiful national park in the California Sierras.

My fiancée Isabel and I happened to arrive in the primetime season for viewing waterfalls—late May in early spring. Naturally we had to stop at nearly every one we could, and eventually found ourselves at the famous Bridalveil Falls.[7]

With a short trail that follows alongside a shy creek, bubbling along, you begin to hear the intimations and rumbling of the falls as you walk, and it only gets stronger

---

[6]   I am here choosing to use the much flawed New English Bible translation, as I was passed down a copy which belonged to my great grandfather, , printed in 1961. This particular verse's translation seems much unharmed.

[7]   Pictured on page 49

The Three

with each step, and as each tourist comes jogging back on the path, soaked from the mist. A little further on you start to feel those puffs of cool mist peeling off of the fall's 617-foot-drop. Then, rounding a corner marked by a massive and impossibly slippery rock, you find yourself at the trail-end, just twenty yards from where the water thunders down against the rocks. From the moment I felt that gentle mist, to the moment of looking at my Isabel, drenched standing next to me, I couldn't wipe the smile off of my face. I doubt I will ever taste clearer air, or feel as deeply cleansed as I was when breathing in that misty Sierra water all the way to my bones. For a moment at least, it was just Isabel and I with our arms open to the mist and the grand Bridalveil showering us. The moment was just all there—completely. It was so whole and clear and succinct and self-evidently *one*. In that moment I felt of the same process as my surroundings, and thus had no reservations of submission to the utter sensitivity of the moment. Consequently, I will remember that moment forever.

———

Some folks keep themselves very busy and shut off such that they simply leave no room for exploration—to wonder about God and the miraculous fact of existence. Even though such things seem set away as abstract irrelevancies, they feel an especially prudent topic in our time. It seems we may be living in a moment of time sometimes called a bifurcation—essentially a word saying, "the pressure is at capacity, and something is going to give, one way or another"—moments in history of revolution, industrialization, the birth of the Internet and World Wide Web, Nazi ideology, etc. Moments of massive change expected to dramatically impress upon the butterfly effect of existence.

This is not to say the search for meaning has stopped universally in our society, only changed course, and perhaps medium and language, during a process of consistent evolution. This is why I am so excited about the artists I mentioned here, and all the many others spreading their God and good news, for, as these things go, the only constant is change. Hopefully we are able to retain and revive the vitality in our present society for this yearning for union, seen in St. Thomas' words: "Man's ultimate happiness consists solely in the contemplation of God." We might use these words to reconnect with one another on the basis of one unifying "end" to our collectively dependent existence.

Currently, I am in the midst of reading Alan Watts' 1950 book *The Supreme Identity* where he references those words of St. Thomas, and he points out that without a unifying philosophy of man's purpose and 'end,' we cannot be a unified society, and I could not agree more. We have to get on the same page and try to gain some sort of clarity with one another, some sort of understanding and levelheadedness. Pure, deep empathy. By this I do not mean one universal religion, creed, or what have you, but *positive* awareness of relativity, and the futility of trying to snuff out what you don't understand in the world. Love and understanding, rather than fear and aggression. Making meaningful again those hippie sort of ideals that have been so scoffed at, overused, misunderstood, and consequently no longer regarded as sincere, unique, or revolutionary in any sense. They have lost all their power by over-saturation and misuse.

What is needed, truly, is a revival of sincerity—with our words, our actions, and our beliefs. Anything else is a continuation of the same vicious circle that has led us and *is* leading us toward the destruction of our planet, the animal kingdom, and our very humanheartedness. We are utterly... disconnected! How ironic in the Age of Information and the Internet.

I suppose the thing I am dancing around is our wanting for a different state of mind; of being. I am here using wanting in the proper way of "to lack" (i.e. if you are hungry, you are left 'wanting' food because you lack it). After all, proclaiming that anyone *need* or ought to do something isn't very compelling, and is indeed not what would fix such a situation as we find ourselves in now.

We are, in fact, simply lacking a certain unity in our common state of mind, and in that way are truly wanting of it. We *want* by way of the aforementioned definition to lack, and also in the fact that there is indeed a revival in the interest of changing states of consciousness happening *now*. Rather than material gain or temporal pleasure, we are showing our want, by lacking, and by action. One could perhaps name this a second hippie generation if they would like, but we have now altogether new capabilities for organization and communication and are consequently an entirely different breed, as it were, with entirely different possibilities.

For a start in this direction, you might begin to reclaim the liveliness of *this* life—for your Self, and for the people around you. Really, sincerely jump into this persona you are—follow your passions and play your part! for the next act is closing in.

The creative power of this instant will become self-evident upon realizing that, indeed, this very instant is all there is—every moment a plunge into the unknown, new, and created world. A new world begging for the courageous.

I'll never be back alive
I'm going out to see

"God is watching, so give him a good show."

maya

my thoughts on how we make sense of the world, particularly in regards to apprehension and ignorance towards foreign religion.

E. H. Parker, in his *Studies in Chinese Religion*, said this, on the common prejudice we hold toward a mysterious and foreign religion:

> *"It is simply a question of education; not only of book-learning; but also of good roads, travel, commerce, interchange of thought, kind treatment, and reasonable concession on our own side."*

Reasonable concession on our own side might be what we are most lacking in our day-to-day associations. We are under a profound illusion, thinking that *our* facts are sitting somewhere superior to everyday reality, and that if we were to consent to loosening our grasp on certain fundamental ideas to engage in such interchange of thought, we might feel insecure, and shaken to our foundation.

Many choose, therefore, to constrict the potential of our human experience only to what can be neatly controlled, documented, and understood—by themselves or people they highly trust. This state of mind can too easily be identified as the characteristic trait of our present world—a world of busyness for the sake of busyness, of going on to keep going on *better*; of the relentless controlling and restriction of things that ought not be controlled or restricted, and the evermore precise and intricate examinaion of all living things. This in turn leads to more intricate and controlling technology, used to exploit, as we deem our right, the lower species and generally 'dumb' environment, which could never keep going were we not here to save it.

This world of ours, in all of its interrelation and complexity, seems at times almost incomprehensible, and is so disregarded and runs unnoticed, by the average person in their day-to-day. The breadth and scope of human knowledge and experience increases exponentially as the days go by. It feels as if there is just not enough time to do everything that we want to do, to read every book we would like to read, and to learn all that we would like to learn. How many times have you heard lately, or thought to yourself that, "Time is flying"? This distorted sense of the passage of time *seems* normal and natural, but only to us living within that very world which prompts it. That world, it is apparent, is the same one of social media, of a solidified and literal around the clock news and propaganda cycle, and more people living than the world has ever seen. There is a lot going on, and more people than ever doing it all; time is after all measured by (or against) the amount of 'events' that happen *within* it, so it seems that our hyper-aware and thus hyper-sensitive society is aware and sensitive to a positively complex and record-breaking amount of events, and is so moving at a record pace toward all ends—and to no end.

The measurement we use for time is shrinking, noticeably, from years, months, weeks, days, and now minutes when describing travel from one location to another. The same sort of evolution and shrinkage of 'spaces' between events has happened also with communication and technology. Smart-phones, surging vehicle and transportation efficiency, and our modern sense of comfortability are all relatively brand new in the human experience. These circumstances seem to be, as a side effect, cutting up the perception of our experience into an incalculable amount of slices, and consequently the tempo of our era has shifted, becoming jarring and intrusive, rather than sensuous and yielding—a kind of societal techno, in lieu of natural rhythm and poetry.

We see the ramifications of this societal attitude all around us now. Watts says in his *Supreme Identity*:

> *"..our age is one of frustration, anxiety, agitation, and addiction to 'dope'... This 'dope' we call our high standard of living, a violent and complex stimulation of the senses.."*

That was written fairly recently in 1951. A person today might read that however only to shrug their shoulders respectfully, and proceed to set the book down in order to watch TV in any one of the increasing possible places in their household; or to engage in a more personal experience with the constantly-chiming smart-phone or tablet, ever titillating you out of focus in the present moment. And I say all of this with full knowledge that I am among you! I am trapped as well in a vortex of screens I can't seem to escape at times. Social media and smart-phones are a massive social experiment playing out before us. An experiment in which we truly have no idea how it will conclude, or how it will change our minds—however that *is* what it's doing.

This unconscious refusal to understand, and failure to really take in the full meaning, is a confusion between intellectual knowledge and actual experience. One may read something they know to be sided with, and still act a completely contradictory way because their mind, in the first place, is split *as* they are receiving the information. Thinking so, they are, in a literal sense, not fully here and not fully experiencing themselves or the information. Split into one half that does and a separate side that ought to, they are taken completely by the illusion of the higher self versus the lower self. This timeless dichotomy has been novelized in several different stories by one of my favorite authors, Hermann Hesse, whose mind like mine is almost obsessively preoccupied with the exploration of this struggle.

This is what *maya* means, anyway: illusion. But it can

also mean magic. For me, maya began by meaning illusion; a temporal world of things, meant eventually to fall away, revealing at last the Final Self. Understanding the world as such lets you in, only slightly, to the secret.

Eventually, maya may come to be understood to represent a self-evident magic; of and within the world, in its web of illusions and revelations; a cosmic design, mapping out no journey in particular. No longer a world that ought to be nicer, healthier, more pretty, or any other thing distinct from other things, for it becomes sufficient in and of its own existence. And, yes! This would still include the healthier, the nicer, the more pretty as well, but would not hold them with exclusivity, ignoring the gratuitous, the harsh, or the well-worn.

Maya is this world in its duality and, *because of that*, also in its togetherness. As the classic question goes, adapted from the original poem by Alfred Lord Tennyson, "Is it better to have loved and lost or to never have loved at all?" The obvious, sober-minded answer is that yes, it is of course worth it to love, knowing full well of its risk of loss, betrayal, and heartbreak. Likewise it is better to experience this world in its duality of joy and pain, rather than to never have experienced it at all. Our inherent knowledge of this answer, even if we care not to admit it in our moments of bitterness, is a sign of the unconscious wisdom that we have not yet forgotten— knowledge that the only true constant in the universe is change, that is, the interplay of black/white, positive/negative, yin/yang, and its importance in creating the life we live. Upon contemplation, the thought of this interplay becomes simply and profoundly: love for All of It.

Seeing through this illusion of finality in duality (an inherently contradictory thought) without ever having left the comfort of your own mind and its preconceptions, such an idea as the beauty of maya and this different state of understanding might seem reductive, pantheistic, or even nihilistic. However, the only thing that a state of mind that is all-right dissolves is a fog of dissociation from the *wholeness* of reality. For, seeing that the world need not be any thing apart from what it is now, in its completeness, you can, without the anxiety, dive completely into any task you choose at this free moment. This maya, this word I deem philosophical, is not to say that it is a waste of time to try to make the world a better place, but only that the very sentence by its conventional structure implies that "I" and "We" are going to change this thing called "World". In reality it is all of one process, pure action and experience, not the symbols for them in words, plans, egos, and most prudently, anxieties. Although seeming inconsequential, the subtle implications of these tricks we play on ourselves really do come to mean a lot.[1]

Maya is, then, the illusory world of things. With a hard 'G'. This ThinG and that thinG, said almost with a low strum of a guitar on the G, like, "thinGGgguuuuuhhhhh", emphasizing the inherent separation and restriction of life when words are taken too seriously—as if they actually mean separation. It is likewise true with this *I*dea and that *I*dea, "because its m*i*ne after all!"

It might be easy after this to slip into a severe relativism and to say that, "Since words and ideas are supposed to be nothing but illusion, then I guess nothing *really* matters?" But that would be wrong. Maya as the illusion of the world (the illusion of seeing it as a mere conglomeration of things) is simply a fact that one might benefit to recognize from time to time; a token of contemplation, like *memento mori*—Latin for 'remember that you have to die'.

These sorts of contemplative phrases are not a negation of reality, of th*i*ngs on the one hand or of life on the other, but a reminder of that dastardly 'other side' that Jung called our shadow, and an effort toward empathetic understanding of it.[2] For we need always to remind ourselves that if an idea or concept such as even death, being so basic in its nature, were to be ultimate and above all others it must be the end of all ends (and to believe that it is "just black" after

---

[1]   Ref: *Framespotting,* Laurence & Alison Matthews (2014)

[2]   Empathy here is to mean simply, as E H Parker guided us, *"reasonable concession on your own side"*, thereafter gaining a better understanding of the situation as a whole, and acting accordingly.

death is pessimism, plainly, and simply unimaginative).

And so finality just cannot be found in thought or words, as they can very easily lead you in circles of concept forever. For certain, words themselves cease to mean much of anything when death arrives, but this is not evidence of a terrible void when the time finally comes, only a completely incomprehensible other side waiting to be explored at its proper moment, refusing the probing of even description and knowledge.

To actively recognize your own relative understanding of things is to gain the capacity for an important empathy and understanding toward any other illusory ideas springing from the world and people around you. Ideas that once might have left you feeling averse to and thus defensive, and reflexive. You instead become completely focused on each moment and quit trying to predict a future that constantly refuses prediction. Rather than getting caught up, literally tangled until strangulation with anxiety, in the ideas of the future or past, you reflect them back out like a mirror—taking them in completely, but as they leave your gaze you are released from any hold they might have had on you. Words begin to take their rightful place as secondary sources to the primary, immediate reality of life and understanding and meaning itself.

It's strange—we might assume the opposite to happen: that upon knowing of only the illusory security brought to us by ideas, and even of ideal morals, it might cause chaos, or some sort of personal existential crisis. On the contrary, it leads to the capability for a deeper, more sincere caring and appreciation for the very reality underlying the many forms of maya: all ideas, all commendations, all ego. Maya, in its magical sense, could also be seen then as a sort of beatific design; a design made up of all the intersections between the myriad of lines that people draw to define their world. A design made up of overlapping illusions of every type: illusions of a good life, of success, of our life purpose as worker bees and problem solvers, as servants, as daughters, as parents, of money, fame, of evil, or of ego. In their entirety, these illusions make up the human experience as it is felt through relationships and the various types of union briefly mentioned in the previous chapter. The beatific design of relativity, I might call it, if I didn't have the much more beautiful name in *maya*.

Maya: the magic of the world, is the vast, interrelated subjective experiences of each and every living thing in the all encompassing now-moment we call Existence; and to my ears, now, the Tao.

This has been preparation for the basis of my point, which is that the fear of another religion is inconsequential at best, and violently repressive at worst. People predictably do not like admitting that what they feel is fear, so they often call it courage instead: "...the courage to stand up to Islam," usually attributing the source of courage to their own respective religious God.

The problem here is that the vision of God is limited and not at all living up to the host of 'omni-'s attributed to him. To admit that more than one religion exists is beside the point—there are many, even if you were to exclude the obscurities of some Native American and indigenous myth, and things like the Bahai'i faith, or even Scientology.

To conflate a system of religion as actually representative in literal terms of a universal God is simply a disservice and confusion of the whole concept. Doing so, you make him your God, as if you had a choice in the ultimate being the Ultimate. God is, by nature, beyond all thinGs (with that strumming 'G' again), and beyond all possession as *I*dea. His beyond-ness might be described or seen in several ways, and however useful, they too are things, tools, and not really representative.

These ways of understanding are, in the West: analogical, and in the East: experiential and contemplative. As seen through Christianity, God is a potter breathing life into his mechanical, inert creations, and he is the Lord Creator over them, dispensing rage, love, justice, and wrath at his will. He is the Primary Mover, and this idea is approached by science from a different direction in the Newtonian idea of one thing pushing second thing, *necessarily* producing third result—known as "billiard ball causation".

This way of intaking the world, though, used alone, forces many things to be misunderstood, and makes others seem improbable or impossible, simply by the error of setting our consciousness to the insurmountable task of lining one thing after another in thought and speech, and insisting it cannot be changed. This reduces the incredible, quantum, algebraic amount of variables involved in any given moment of our existence to basic arithmetic, and yet we continue to attempt it—claiming all the while that by mere persistence it is courageous.

It is not so much courageous as it is simply habitual and inherited. We say, "This is what I am aware of, so this is what is true." But that is not wholly so, and for some reason we are only able to admit this when pushed and even then do not really *feel* it. This goes back to the confusion between intellectual knowledge and experiential wisdom; between knowing the world as thing/thing and experiencing it as maya; as idea and not reality; as the sound "pitcher" having more meaning than a full container of water.

It seems as though we no longer have the capacity, or patience, for the mysterious. It is no small fact that the hyper-awareness of our society is continuously—right now— affecting the collective consciousness of us all, and thus guiding the course of our future. Due to this hyper-sensitivity and awareness, everything seems exposed with nothing left to imagination. In that lull of intrigue, imagination withers too weak to make this game of life feel worth the struggle, and our deepest anxieties seem to thrive on the fear that comes in turn. We feel exposed, seemingly existing in a true-to-life Orwellian society, completely aired out of all secrets; all the more so as the security of words and ideas crumble beneath us. This is not to our despair though, for the feeling was misplaced to begin with, and recognizing this, the creative moment again begins to come alive.

This feeling of complete anxiety, permeating all corners of our mind, would transfer quite easily to our handling of religion. We assume that all of the spiritual information that can be unearthed *is*, or at the very least, is just around the corner from being so. It seems easy enough to simply take stock of all available options and to ask impatiently, "Well what's the best one? —the most established, tried-and-true, fully developed?" And this line of questioning is itself just around the corner from adopting the tendency to sort out which beliefs are 'bad ones' and which are to be tolerated and taught to our children. This decision is of course completely subjective, and the broad ideals are left entirely undefined, for "what is chaos to the fly is order to the spider." What is enlightenment to one is morally repugnant to another. The enduring problem is that we fail to recognize the ever-presence of relativity.

Relativity itself is seen in a very drab way to us, a so-called 'realistic and practical society'—as either being the excuse for lawbreakers, or an inconsequential concept completely. Such a concept becomes subject to the "objective" and ultimate law of whatever that individual sees as his highest authority, usually some sort of God, king, or a hybrid of the two. In this present social understanding of God, I see the prudent missing link to be in our apprehension of non-duality, or rather misapprehension completely.

As an aside, I feel that life itself should be felt as completely fluid in its most basic nature. The implication of this is a certain lightheartedness not usually felt when life is perceived as a singularly life-or-death, survival-for-survival scenario.[3] This fluidity carries with it certain varying levels of

---

[3]   If it needs definition, life here is to mean the very experience we are having right now. While I write and you read, our thoughts and actions can be *played* with in a very exciting way. You can scream if you'd like. You could light this book on fire, or read through to the end. You can choose to make your eyes go cross, or to do nothing at all. You can do

depth as well. Keeping in mind that the only universal constant is change, there should be no objection to the sentiment that life and its ideas can be 'played with' like clay or dough—made into whichever shape or form fulfills the needs of a moment.

To ensure clarity it should be noted once again that non-duality does not mean 'both' or 'neither'—it would be closer to a clumsy word like "itness." So, when speaking on religion and non-duality, I do not mean Western theology and philosophy is better than Eastern, or vice versa, nor do I mean them to be equal (as if I 'didn't see color' in regards to race, and was fighting ignorance with more ignorance).

Non-dual understanding is acknowledging that *what* exactly 'this' or 'that' *is* matters less than the reality doing the 'thising' or 'thating'. You are no longer committed, for lack of a better word, to this or that. You find yourself in a completely new world as it appears to you in the universally new moment, able to entertain and see the multitude of sides to every situation.

Non-duality ultimately is itself an attempt to shut you up about it. For to say, "this is good," "this is bad," "this is both," or "this is neither" is all saying too much, and also nothing at all. Buddhists would again call it 'putting legs on a snake' because, if one truly understood non-duality they wouldn't bother trying to explain those four points of view plus their own—they would simply accept the fact of many points of view, and continue to act according to whatever the pressing situation demanded. Buddhists say about Zen:

> *"Zen spirituality is not talking about God while peeling potatoes. Zen spirituality is just to peel the potatoes."*

A new way of acting the knowledge instead of theorizing the knowledge comes about quite quickly. Separation between

whatever you'd like as the natural constrictions of nature and body allow. Life, then, is your immediate experience, including also the 'watcher' of that experience, and the supposed organizer of your thoughts and plans.

action and idea dissolves, not as if you must formulate in words a concept, in order for it to be true. When the ancients thought the sun ran away below the horizon, they simply did not have the scientific words or language to describe what had been, in reality, happening for millennia and would continue happening for millennia after. They did have their myth, however both myth and science, in language, have no *real* effect on the underlying 'real world,' regardless of our desires and our constructs of what "ought to be", or even what we deem 'Universal Rules.'

Those things that we use to define our world—determining thus what we pull and learn from the world—may be called primaries for ease. 'Primaries' are really just a particular way to describe relativity and non-duality in the same breath, and from the point of view of an individual.

I might say that my primary is philosophy or religion, although that may change depending on an individual stimulation of the senses—including common and intellectual sense. When I watch a movie or listen to music or read a book, I extract information along whichever specific avenue is piqued by whatever specific instigation. Sometimes I find that my extraction is somewhat based in reality, and sometimes I find it is completely my own extrapolation.

A contemporary example of the former is in *Star Wars*. The Force is so obviously for me a metaphor for the Tao from eastern philosophy, and when Obi-Wan, Yoda, and Luke 'ghost' into the Force, it is obviously a metaphor for enlightenment and escape from samsara (the wheel of birth and death).[4]

These thoughts have been, to a degree, validated for me through reading about George Lucas' relationship with the works of Joseph Campbell, a scholar of comparative mythology. Lucas at one point or another drew inspiration for his now iconic saga in the writings of Campbell—particularly *Hero With A Thousand Faces*. Campbell was by no means stuck in any mythological rut. He authored a series of books titled

---

[4]   As an aside, their returning to the world of form as Force-ghosts, is in its own sense, their bodhisattva return.

Maya

The Masks of God, detailing religious traditions worldwide. His works became so personally influential to Lucas' saga that Lucas invited Campbell and his wife to his newly completed Skywalker Ranch for a screening of the original trilogy. This relationship is an affirmation for me of my own reflections on Lucas' saga—its meaning and potential as a commentary on real life, and not stuck in the frame of being *only* a science fiction "space opera".

On the other hand, I have extracted copious amounts of inspiration and insight from innumerable artists in music, who I have listed and spoke of briefly in the previous chapter. My thoughts on the excerpts from those songs are, I am quite sure, unique to me or at least to this particular sort of primary. I imagine that others who intake the world with an interest they cannot shake in philosophy and the exploration of the mind cannot help but extrapolate meaning in a similar way. Still others might use music therapeutically or innocently, and in these ways may not think too much into their entertainment—simply using it as an escape from whatever is ailing them.

These primaries develop in an indecipherably subtle way from all of the micro-associations, influences and experiences throughout our lives, and because of that go largely undetected by even ourselves.

> *"..our age is one of frustration, anxiety, agitation, and addiction to 'dope'… This 'dope' we call our high standard of living, a violent and complex stimulation of the senses.."*

Sixty-eight years later, this quote still rings true. Regarding the former half, of our frustration, anxiety and agitation, I believe these feelings are first and foremost true of us. Secondly, I believe we take them out on one another as humans as commonplace because we feel deeply that "I am this, and you are that." I believe we all feel so frustrated with one another because we have lost the ability to understand ourselves as connected. Of the latter half, of our *"standard of living, a violent and complex stimulation of the senses,"* I agree as well.

It feels as though we are completely and consistently distracted and preoccupied. Why, after all, should we take the time to understand one another when we can so easily get the answer from our ever-chiming electronics, or the hour-by-hour, minute-by-minute updates from our social media. Those things at least tend to agree with us, and we with them. But in the end they will fail us, or worse—bore us, and we will be left looking around aimless, trying to adjust our eyes to a world we no longer recognize, and to a Maya completely stripped of its magic.

Maybe this has happened already? Have we become so distracted with the technological and the faux-social that, as we encounter the natural once again, we simply find it boring? Our social climate, suffocating the population with endless entertainment-propaganda, undeniably fits the description as Watts put it—and how can we not expect to see negative reverberations from such a longstanding state of affairs?

If you whip a long wire or rope, suspended between two poles, the waves and reverberations last longer than the actual whipping—the cause. As it happens we are seeing the reverberations of past generations' violence on the natural in just the same way. We may not have done the whipping, but we are attached to its fate, and it is coming back to us nonetheless, and we have to deal with it as it comes. And we *are* trying to do so. Carbon taxes, animal conservation and extinction awareness, widespread recycling, electric cars, solar and wind energy technologies, a massive growth in the popularity and accessibility to veganism, and more ideas pouring in from our younger generations every day.

I am at heart optimistic for this coming age, and toward our coming of age creators and visionaries. I am excited for the building of a new world and a new mindset—and most of all for a rediscovery of maya, properly, as appreciation for the beauty of life.

"I wish
I was what I was
when I wished
I was what I am"

tao

my thinking on the world, after having learned what little I verily have.

prelude

a poem & prose, unedited

I don't know how
exactly to say this
but listen:

I think there is a desperate need for a new empathy today.
I think there is a desperate need for a new sacrifice.
A new compassion, a new love, and… a new philosophy.
A new mind.

Who do you suppose is to give us these things?
You?
Me?
I?

Well . . .
You are you and I am Me
yet also . . .
I feel 'I' and You feel 'I'
So. . . it seems . . .
(something new and something daring)
I need to listen,
and
I need to do differently.

•

Well, I feel the need for such an overhaul because we as a people are so utterly disconnected with the way things are. There is no longer any concern for where our food comes from and how it gets to us. We virtually ignore all the indigenous peoples of the world, have no reverence for the land we live on and simply use it. We have fallen to the delusion that we exist from 'womb to tomb' for the sole purpose of labor and problem solving. We have…disconnected…from the way things are. Throughout all of this we have begun to isolate ourselves deeper and deeper into our six-inch LED screens. If they were the Baby Boomers, and I am a Millennial, these today are in danger of being the Screen Savers.

Incidentally, this period of time is all too easy to talk poorly of. Really, it's just the natural symptom and consequence of existence becoming more complex. With every baby born, every technology innovated, every disease cured, every star seen. Increasing the complexity, in tandem with this Tech Era, is the speed at which everything seems to be happening at. Or rather, the speed at which things are able to be known to be happening. With things like social media, everything is solved, discussed, and aired out in an instant. This has its value for certain, and is not *necessarily* a negative attribute that I'm describing—only a part of a fact.

Indeed it is a sentiment of age that "life is flying by," but it is increasingly becoming a universal observation. Things are happening faster, and to keep pace, people want the next thing faster. Consequently, attention spans of people today are next to nil. Having everything aired out in such a public way as the Internet has dimished our capacity for surprise. We are heading toward a day where the only smiles will be for more and more elaborate displays of multicolored LEDs. We care not to wonder because, why not simply Google it? Why read a carefully researched article, or participate in a long conversation, when I can glance at a tweet? Why go talk to someone struggling when I can watch it here on TV?

Why bother?

For the LIFE of it.

I feel that people no longer engage with LIFE in an immediate, direct way. While walking down the street, just kneel down and place your palm on the ground. *Feel* the people walking around you. You are there. Be in it. When you are listening to someone speak, make that voice your whole world. Picture the words in your mind's eye, then reply. Avoid just saying words back *at* them. Converse. When you're smoking a joint or opening a can of beans, be so completely into these everyday activities that they take on their rightful weight as complete miracles of existence. How wild it is to be anything at all! Be present in all moments that gift themselves to you. YOU, reading this.

It is profoundly disconcerting watching this sort of fog creep in over people, preventing anything meaningful from happening and preventing things from being reflected upon. Folks lose all knowledge of the spirit of life and resort, by default, to drudgery and habit. We are living in a world of antitheses: of freedom, of care, of empathy, understanding, of humanheartedness…and of leisure…

RESIST. For the LIFE of it . . .

Now, I would like to write about my newfound excitement and optimism for life—feeling awake to what's going on. I write here not to proclaim that I am sitting pretty in such an awake mindset, but instead to share in my amazement at the experience of it, even briefly. I am here not to say just one thing or one truth, but to open a broader window to the mind—particularly my mind.

Any life, filled with all the experiences that it would have, can be chosen and narrated in such a way that it may come to analogize certain universal principles and truths and, like Zen says of peeling potatoes, you do not *always* need to point at it and affirm in words a meaning that is already there and self-evident.

Knowing this, I have come to love novels, particularly *The Greek Passion* by Nikos Kazantzakis, and *The Glass Bead Game (Magister Ludi)* by Hermann Hesse. I have also come to appreciate the form of novel itself for its leading ability to convey truths in a way like poetry—not by saying the point, but alluding to it with a smirk that says, "Youuu know, you see it! Keep reading.. but *you know.*"

What I intend with this chapter is an explanation of the way in which life has changed for me after discovering The Three—an altogether different way of thought. However,

Tao

I can't figure out exactly *how* to describe such a complex and continuous 'event'.

With *On My Self*, I decided on poetry, but here I feel a pull to simply talk about my life as an expression of its change and course. There are times that I wish I could accurately describe what I was truly like at an early age, but I can see myself only with the eyes I have on today. This may therefore have a strong tone of reflection, centered around that which is reflected—my life.

I began this chapter by talking about novels and their capability for higher expression because although I may speak, literally, on my life only, the analogies that may be drawn are adaptable to the specifics of almost any other scenario. I say this in fear of people reading on only one dimension— of seeing only my first-person perspective and so saying that it is selfish and self-deluded. This book, in truth, may very easily be seen as selfish—simply because it is *strictly* about what I am thinking, and reading and seeing and hearing and remembering.

But if you allow yourself a peek elsewhere, out of that tunnel vision, you may find that you relate to it; and by relating to it you begin not to notice which pronoun or tense is being used—you find yourself just digging it in your own terms. And to dig, to understand, is not always to agree with, but to *be with*.

Having said all this, I would like to write on whatsoever may come to me when reflecting on the question: "Who are you?"[1]

There is a very small selection of memories that I have retained from the period before my life started to be

---

[1]   Put another way: "What has been your Tao?". Tao can be translated as Way (of nature) or Law (of balance)—both definitions retain a particularly organic meaning. In still other words it might be: how have you grown? What has been your change?

Simply 'Who are you?' is meant not only to elicit a name and occupation, but on a deeper level of understanding, is asking what makes you, *you*—or me, *me*.

filmed. I remember summers. Summers were a time when all our fruit was ripe for picking and I would beg my sister Molly to go picking with me and, if I was lucky, to make a smoothie later with our haul. I remember learning early how to drive a 4-wheeler; my brother Zach had the yellow one, Molly had purple, and my brother Jer had green. I don't recall which of the three I was riding on one particular day when I drove straight *up* a tree, distracted by one of my brothers behind me. The tree grew sideways for its whole life, until being torn out during a landscaping project when I must've been near thirteen.

As I sit here recollecting, I find, too, that some memories have an unclear placement in the line of chronology, simply because of their proximity to the beginning of filming. For in all of its excitement and chaos, it seems to have blurred things. A consistently recurring memory from that earlier time is of my brother Zach and I staging elaborate sort of scenes and battles with *G.I. Joe* figures all around the farm. I remember when we got the miniature *G.I. Joe* brand canoe and I remember the hours in total spent on the other side of a culvert, waiting as Zach sent them cruising my way.[2] I remember climbing trees and 'Base Tag'. I remember our family dog Rocky and before him Vern and Marge, the Westies. I remember the sandbox. And cousins. I remember my mom's garden with her red and yellow tulips, and roses that made me bleed when I 'ran away' to hide near them outside. I remember the tree I would climb to get on the roof of the shed.

I try to remember and retain these memories, and that's it; a way of safely compartmentalizing the 'pure' memories away from those taken over by filming, for I hardly see the connection between some of those early memories

---

[2]   Just the other day, Zach and I, along with my fiancée, his wife Tori, and son Jackson, walked around the same (but very different) farm and came across a healthy creek far out by the forest, with a vibrant sort of green grass growing all over in a patch, and a little sandbar to access it. I thought, "Boy, does this remind me of—" and Zach beat me to it, asking me if I remembered all the hours spent with *G.I. Joes* by that same type of creek.. ..Yes!

and experiences and the person I am today—although I know there is one—because the life and memories that took over have been so domineered by and synonymous with 'filming'. They're of an altogether different league, and seem incomparable. I gauge this not by goodness or badness but in obviousness; and it needs no more explanation.

My parents have always been pretty amazing. They both succeeded in life, making a family, and providing for their kids all that they wanted, within disciplined reason. My dad taught me practical things like how to play chess and how to build a fire, and other sorts of exercises in basic critical thinking that I still carry with me today. He was a captivating storyteller, sitting all of us kids by the fire and telling stories of "dark, windy nights." My mom, always making sure we knew we were loved, supported all of our efforts and hobbies—even coaching all of us kids in soccer during our early years. She instilled in us a very good sense of manners and respect that I find myself appreciating more everyday—a sort of child rearing centered around the Golden Rule.

Above all, I'm just so happy that my parents believed in life enough to have four kids.

My twin brothers, now with their own wives and a daughter and son respectively. My sister, with her own husband and booming life in Spokane. Now I too am entering these open seas of life and have gotten myself engaged to a wonderful beauty of a girl, and begun to pursue a craft. This—the farm, our next generation of family, with its many reverberations—comes due to my parents, their dedication to family, and belief in life. I simply, and greatly, appreciate the work that my parents have done to sculpt the life that my siblings and I have been blessed to live.

By nature of being their child, I am afforded a hindsight view of some of their choices, and so have certain privileges in regards to my opinion of them and their choices. This does not mean that any one of their decisions are strictly wrong and neither that my opinion from my own perspective is strictly right. I do not speak disapprovingly of filming in an effort to reverse their past decision, nor to achieve reparations—but as a fact of my experience.[3]

People who may have watched my family and I for some years may feel that they have their own unique perspective on these decisions and opinions, and they do; however I might describe it as uniquely narrow. The entire concept of reality TV is strange because, as a viewer, you are subscribing to a particular illusion that you are witnessing and being let in on the secrets of the subjects' lives. *In reality*, you are being shown a shallow character and only what someone else approves of, in relation to narrative and talking points. This was my meaning in saying the "Roloff Characters" in the past: not that the real people are characters or deliberately acting; but whichever Roloff you *think* you know is in fact a *shown* character—sculpted specifically to entice and convince you to *keep this channel on*.

Looking back, I think—like everyday discipline which you hate but later come to respect—filming was both awful and a blessing. In its own way it was a good source of strength for varying disciplines and personality traits that I have come to appreciate as I have grown.

My dad was already gaining local celebrity with his amazing construction projects on the farm, such as 'The Ghost Town', 'Molly's Castle', 'the Treehouse', and the 'Jolly Roger' pirate ship, later renamed 'Jolly Mo', after my sister Molly Jo. Because of this local fame and the uniqueness of our family's biology, a production company asked whether our family would like to participate in a reality show of one type or another—their answer is history, of course.

Whatever its original intent, the show turned out to be a great source of awareness for dwarfism and, thirteen years on, there seems to be about a dozen other reality TV shows on the air about little people. This doesn't imply direct causation,

---

[3]   Within this fact, too, there are dimensions. For I cannot say confidently that filming was one thing or another—only that it happened, and that I think on it daily. My expression of these thoughts is no damnation, but a process still unfolding.

only a sense of influence and timing.

As for me, the whole thing didn't matter much in the beginning. I was attending Faith Bible Christian School at the time, which was another daily discipline that I both loved and hated. I received a fantastic education and the blessing of small classrooms and attentive teachers. I also received (likely, I don't really know) around 100 detentions, a handful of suspensions, and finally an expulsion.

I mostly find humor in the memories at this point. I was a hellion—constantly challenging adult authority, often with my fellow black sheep student cohorts. Some of it was downright senseless. At the end of school days they would gather the kids in a sort of auditorium to wait for pick-ups or buses, and on a dare in the 2nd grade, I stood up in the room and just yelled, "fuck". That earned me a talking to, laced with a healthy amount of scripture memorization homework, as well as a detention or two. Most of my other detentions were for menial things like dress code violations or chewing gum. I was just a troublemaker there, with several teacher feuds, and minimal friends.

Truthfully, only one friend remains from that school, although she and I haven't spoken since my expulsion, but I gather that we both consider each other good friends to whom we would help if ever called. A delightful revelation.

After being threatened with expulsion in the eighth grade for low grades and lack of participation, I was told to raise my GPA to at least a 2.0. So in the few weeks before the semester end, I reluctantly completed all my outstanding assignments and homework, raising my GPA to a 2.14 (from a 1.2 or thereabouts). The school administrators graciously allowed me to complete my SAT tests happening that week. Then, they followed through relieving me of my enrollment at their school without further explanation. Alas, my education and my one friend—for those both, I greatly appreciate my time at Faith Bible.

To my luck, they did it at *just* the right time—late enough to eliminate the need to repeat any coursework at public high school the following year, and early enough for me to get an extra two and a half months of summer. I still laugh thinking of Faith Bible these days—not at them, but in appreciation of how things turn out. They really have.

By this time we were about six or seven seasons deep into filming, and the show had really taken off in popularity and scale. I recognize now how blessed I was with the opportunity to travel all over the world following the course of the show—the British Virgin Islands, Australia, Italy, Ireland, France, and various other stateside trips and privileges which I heartily enjoyed. The boon resulted eventually in my dad being able to purchase a neighboring farm, adding nearly ninety acres of land to our own—creating a whole landscape of creative possibilities for himself. The farm became a fantastic wedding venue, leading all of my siblings to get married on the farm, soon followed by myself.

During those early teenage years I was constantly acting out against the show's presence and, in my better moods, would play games with the crew by avoiding them. I'd climb trees and hide while a crew of at least three searched for me, and sometimes literally chased me around the farm trying to reign me in for one of those *detestable* formal interviews.

Speaking of this, I should mention that I have never *intended* ill will toward any particular crew member, save for one.

Only later did it dawn on me the personal strain that my antics may have caused for the crew; they were simply people with a job to do, although that's not quite a solid enough excuse in and of itself. The cameras they were using at that time weighed nearly forty pounds, and the sound equipment likewise, including a five-to-twenty-pound sound boom. In the early days of this cat-and-mouse game I had even the producers chasing me, until they wised up and started lobbying my parents to incentivize my participation.

On the subject of the crew, I have to mention Marcel and Ollie (Oliver), a German father-son duo of sound guys. Both had big bright genuine smiles, always joking and making fun out of whatever situation arose, even when dealing with my dad's micro-producing.[4]

There was also Dan, the Mountain Man,[5] who I remember as being aloof, but kind; a hard worker, but willing to drop it at the expense of being humanhearted. On a popular moment in the show, I was in the forest with Zach and Molly building a fort when all of a sudden I stepped on a nail, grabbing for my foot in pain as Zach ran to help me. Then it cuts to us arriving at the house.

What actually happened was this: I stepped on the nail, my brother had no real clue what to do and, as a kid himself, looked to Dan behind the camera. Seeing Zach's "I have no idea what to do" eyes, and as he began to ask it, Dan quickly set the camera down and provided a reassuring, adult point of view that was enough to draw the panic out of the situation. After that, a semi-official rule was struck down upon Dan's request, saying that the crew may not interfere with the subjects. Common sense and humanheartedness were shown to me, which is why I still remember such moments these years later, even as the crew filtered in and out. The crew members that we did develop relationships with made the whole ordeal of the show worth it—assuming the experience could be priced.

Lastly, there was one particularly agreeable producer who led me to believe that he understood my position as an overwhelmed child. Maybe—*maybe*—his persona, the part he played, was just his own manipulative way of achieving my participation, but I don't think so. He was a genuinely kind, wild Kentuckian, with the best stories and an (almost) unbelievably interesting life; always finding ways to forego the way things 'should be' to make me a little more comfortable, and if he couldn't, at least acknowledging the fact. I consider him a valuable mentor—although we don't speak as often as I might like. I enjoyed his presence as it grew more familiar, and after he left the show for other business, I *really* had

---

[4]   Joke.

[5]   Not an officially agreed-upon nickname.

nearly no other reason to participate.

After almost three years of being outside it though, with a crew all new and foreign to me, I had my 21st birthday party at the farm and unexpectedly saw Marcel. He had the same, *best* smile on his face, and we exchanged how do you do's, and he commented on some piece of writing he had seen of mine that he enjoyed. I was so happy, genuinely, that he appeared to approve of my breaking away from the show. Not that I require the approval of every crew member who I liked, but it was an endearing sentiment that I will remember for some time.

It's not as if I have done some outrageous thing by exiting—it isn't *more* weird to stop participating in a reality TV show than it is to begin one in the first place. Among so many things, I simply did not want this ridiculous thing— reality TV—to use up so much of my time, lest it leave too deep an imprint on my ability to influence the world otherwise; I did not want this imposition to become my identity, and so I rebelled in the manner that I did, and eventually exited the show.

Around this general period of nine to thirteen, I was playing soccer and was pretty good. My mom and brothers were all very much into soccer and instilled in me the same enthusiasm. I played with my brothers on our lawn over countless summer days, on the team for Faith Bible in 7th and 8th grades, and then for Hillsboro Soccer Club. First with my mom and then with Mike Detjen as my coach, who would continue to be my coach for the next five years or so. Mike had been introduced to me as my brothers' coach, and when he saw Jeremy's talent he became a close family friend to all of us, going on to coach the Faith Bible high school team when my brothers were there, as well as working for my dad's company, Direct Access Solutions, in a leading role.

In the last few years a lot of people have commented that Mike seemed like he had been a 'father figure' to me, and I've accepted the label, but mentor would do just as fine. I think the latter carries even more weight—but that isn't really the point. I appreciate Mike's influence on me *a lot*.

On occasion when my mom was busy, Mike drove me to various soccer events and tournaments. Some took place hours away, and he would get me reading *Popular Mechanics* and *Popular Science* out loud during the long drive. I expanded my mind and learned new words from the writing inside those magazines, and even things I didn't fully understand in the moment helped me later as a writer and reader.

Mike was an Intel engineer for several decades, remaining afterwards a very technologically obsessed guy, always first with the Blu-rays and the newest toy robots of the early 2000's; he was the pocket protector type, in the absolute most endearing way. On these mini road trips, and back home, he would set me up on his computer with strategy games, such as *StarCraft*, *Rome: Total War*, and *The Battle For Middle Earth*. I find reasons all the time to credit these habits—of reading the *Popular*s and playing strategy games—as being major influences on my mental development. In other words, what I already know about Mike's influence on me, I find reaffirmed often.

Mike passed away in October of 2008, after collapsing from a cardiovascular complication along the lines of a torn aorta artery. I think I was in fifth grade at the time and I remember every detail of the morning my mom came to my room to tell me that Mike had not made it through his surgery. I don't remember the days afterward very well—only that I skipped school for a few days and was likely very foul to anyone around me. And I cried often.

I remained, largely unconsciously, upset with my mom for a long time because, at the hospital, there was a chance for us kids to go in and see him to say goodbye, and she didn't let me. Likely it was for rational reasons considering my age and lack of exposure to death up until that moment, but the feeling persisted. I realized only later that my suppressed anger was instead misplaced and unaddressed grief.

Mike's influence on me—obvious and subtle—and

all the memories I cherish, cannot be summed up in even one whole book.

I had seen Mike the day prior to his collapse for a 1-on-1 soccer training session, and planned to meet again the following day. He was my regular season coach at the time and after his passing I managed to complete the season with his assistant coach (who I rather disliked). I stopped playing soccer after that and have not returned since—save for a few recreational indoor games. I struggled for a long while about whether that decision would've disappointed Mike, but am sure now that it wouldn't have. He might even be proud.

Although I certainly wish that things didn't *have* to transpire the way that they did, I am grateful for all of the time and lessons I learned from him nonetheless. And I still miss Mike.

Turning my attention back to reflect on the filming happening parallel to all of this, I find myself feeling just as contemptuous and bored as ever. Consequently I think I will pass on those details, and talk instead of more recent things, at a quickened pace.

In high school, I had only two romantic relationships, both rather short-lived. The first was innocent enough, however we were complete opposites. The second had its bright spots, but was ultimately toxic for us both, and luckily ended somewhat amicably at a stage primed just so for the two of us to benefit more from the dissolution rather than continuation of the relationship. By then it was junior year, and I had been psychologically checked out of school for years. Not of disinterest in learning, but of scarce opportunity to do so in a public school with most teachers seemingly disinterested in teaching. There was only one teacher that I actually liked, but he later became involved in scandalous affairs on school grounds, consequently losing his position and going to prison.

After losing the teacher to the only two classes I went to, incidentally being psychology and sociology, I left my high school to finish what I felt was an increasingly pestuous stage of compulsory learning by getting a GED instead. I passed the exam with flying colors and then began internally exploring what I wanted in life.

During this time, I finally reconnected with a longtime, however distant, friend from high school, Izzy, who was in the class above mine. The few times we did converse, I was trying to figure out why *she* was talking to *me,* because the assumed norms of public school said that she shouldn't be: she was a grade up, beautiful and popular, and I was the new kid, duly isolated from my reputation of being on TV. After all, it turned out that we weren't so different. She happened to ride my bus on Wednesdays, and so I saw her then, too. She would always sit beside me, and soon from this connection we began texting intermittently and eventually, everyday.

We never did arrange to see each other in person beyond school and those bus rides, but I remember watching her get off at her stop, so close to my own, and trying to figure out where she lived. Unbeknownst to me, she lived only a stone's throw away from my own family farm, and my family dog Rocky often ran away to her house to meet with their girl dog Osa. Two kids on either side of the train tracks.

She graduated at the same time that I dropped out in order to get a GED and, nearly every night that summer, we just as well experienced some type of time travel. One minute I was picking her up from her house and the next, we were two hours from home, parked somewhere on a service road with the sunrise coming up and the birds starting to chirp. We did that for a long while, and never ran out of things to talk about. We just enjoyed one another completely, and still do!—as she is now my fiancée, Isabel Sofía Garretón. To this day, our favorite thing to do is driving new roads together.

I turned eighteen and, having dated only a few months at the time, we decided to move into an apartment together—with our two dogs Moose and Luna. We have been virtually inseparable in the four years since, and I'm eager for a lifetime more.

Tao

For when Izzy joined my life, so did all of the loving, artistic, and magical people that surrounded her. Her mother Toni for one, continues to inspire me in her activism and love for others in life. She dedicated her career to teaching English to non-native speakers at Portland Community College, but it went beyond that—she *truly* cared for her students and their families, and did so for no other reason than the love of it—the goodness of it. It is one trait among many that she has handed down to her daughter. Izzy's brothers are also constant sources of learning and reflection; Tomás in his music and Nico in his selflessness and generosity. I am still hearing new stories from Toe and Nico's travels around the Americas and I hope I do forever because they're a gift. Adam & Emma, Scott, Sleepy, Anthony, Kiwi, Jake, Lex, and literally countless others seem to have been gathered around the magic and warmth of this family, and I am happy to be one of them. Even having regretfully never had the chance to meet Toni or Tomás in this life, I feel the reverberations of their influence and magic all over the place, and they live on in those they have impacted.

After a year of living together, Izzy and I moved to Arcata, California, which we absolutely loved. A town of less than eighteen thousand, five minutes from the closest beach, twenty minutes from the famous Avenue of the Giants and also dog-friendly; it was absolutely our type of town— perfect. Arcata and living there became a sort of incubational place: Izzy discovered her talent as an artist and a poet, and I discovered my desire to write. We both came out of it with similar entrepreneurial aspirations, and the passion to execute them. We lived there almost exactly a year.

I never would have imagined I'd be where I am, with who I am, today, but I am positively thankful and consequently more faithful. Izzy has tempered my wildness and anger with grace and love, while also rocking her own life. We are sufficiently different that we learn and grow constantly from one another, but not so different that we are always opposed. Somehow, the two of us, who had no patience for shenanigans within a relationship, found each other. We both had examples in our life of how to care for and behave in a relationship and how not to behave, and also both retained a strong desire to create a family of our own, which is to say we both had great mothers and complicated families.

It was while we were living in Arcata that the idea to write my first book developed slowly. Firstly, by my reading of Hermann Hesse's magnum opus *The Glass Bead Game,* and the poem within, written by the main character, Joseph Knecht:

> *Our days are precious but we gladly see them going*
> *If in their place a thing more precious growing;*
> *A rare, exotic plant, our gardener's heart delighting;*
> *A child whom we are teaching, a booklet we are*
> *writing.*

Secondly, by Izzy's brother Nico encountering a newsstand of self-published booklets from various local poets and writers and handing some off to Izzy and I. The two events in conjunction acted with many others to spur this most recent desire to write something—at the least, to see how it felt. Nearly a year on now, I find that I am everything *but* disappointed.

In July 2017, I wrote my first booklet that I titled *Verbing*(道 流); it was both an incredibly exciting and also underwhelming experience. During the writing of it, which was no more than a month or two—I knew it would be short— and merely introductory to what I would write about later on. However I didn't realize how quickly the urge to write again would come. After releasing it, I almost instantly felt that it was inadequate, for I had so many other thoughts to add; so much left unexpressed. That was part of my process, though, to almost purposefully leave it unedited and as coherently raw as I could. I didn't know what was going to happen or come to me after putting it out, but it 'worked.'

Now, I am nearing the end of writing *this* book, and I have no idea what is next for me. This family-building, life-building stage is right upon me now, and so being the present-becoming-future, I cannot seem to reflect on it, or make it yet a part of the *answer* to who I am. There is action, then reflection/contemplation, then expression, and to write about what is right under my feet would be premature.

I have attempted to paint a picture by merely outlining, sketchily, that which I wish to show: my nature as observer, and my enjoyment to the utmost in *thinking* about what I observe. 'Thinking about' seems too dry and limited though, and so no doubt contemplating would be more accurate, although it still carries a certain stuffy tone.

I was always encouraged in school to recognize and hone in my writing skills, and I have, for the most part, kept to myself for a long time. The contents of my mind are a mystery to even the closest to me—not because I am withholding from contempt, but because true observation and contemplation never stops and I have been preoccupied for years with a massive amount of information that fills my mind and now my books. It seems I have reached capacity, because I find now that I have no stronger desire than to write.

I have no particular interest in recounting specific events as much as I do for how events can affect a state of mind, how they *do* and *are* affecting states of mind—I have interest in observing a practical (real) thing, reflecting it against the appropriate themes (concepts) in my own mind, creating an abstraction, and then contemplating on whether or not the result would affect the present, and how. This linear and blocky way I am communicating is seeming to fail me in properly indicating the extreme and positive energy I feel from this outlet of release in writing; this failing is not, however, due to the medium of communication, but due I suppose to the "you just had to be there" factor. Or in this case, "you've just got to try it for yourself."

Tao

If nothing else, in my life and in my writing, I'd like to encourage people to explore the depths of being human (that is, to explore philosophy). Which is by no means to imply that I have completed my own exploration, as a vacation which I highly recommend, but in the spirit of this, from Augustine:

> *"For man, there is no cause to philosophize; except in order to be happy."*

Without question I have found this to be true during my coming of age, for through philosophizing I have found my passion, my faith, my peace, my confidence, my family, and every other blessing I count today; a path on which I will continue until called elsewhere, if ever.

Tao

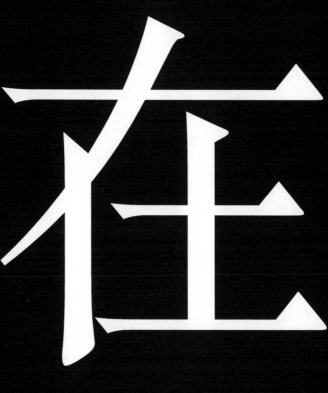

supplement

On Watts
(and keeping him in the basement)

I wrote an essay some time ago entitled *Keeping Mr. Watts in the Basement*—about the writer, philosopher, and speaker Alan Watts—and I would like to revisit it here.

I wrote that piece due to my almost daily struggle of feeling like a tag-along to his work and worldview. I have tried to reconcile this feeling within myself but it persists, and so I write about it again, in defense of myself.

I maintain that I am not in fact copying Watts as much as I am simply, gratefully, drawing from him. This is due to the sincere connection I feel with his experience and the words he used while speaking of the world and its religions, as well as his attitude as a philosopher.

Watts began as a Christian (actually Episcopal, though an easy jump). He attended a Catholic school in England and was raised in a Catholic society. Somewhere along the line, due to a number of influences, he became fascinated with Eastern philosophy—Buddhism in particular. In his early 20's he found his way to Chicago, joining the Episcopal Church there and, eventually, becoming an ordained priest. He was *in* it.

I have learned, after spending some time with Watts' eldest son Mark, now with his own family and kids, that his father did this with the conscious intent to change the church from within, by introducing an awareness and acceptance of a certain mystical point of view, so expertly illuminated by Zen and Mahayana Buddhism. In time, he gave up this insurmountable task within the boundaries he was set in order to, among other things, write independently to the public at large—first with *Behold the Spirit* (1950), then with *The Supreme Identity* (1951). Watts had a knack for "writing beautifully the unwritable" (*Los Angeles Times*) and was at the forefront of exposing the West to the culture and philosophy of the Far East. He was able to not only write *about* the Far East but to make it digestible to the people of the West. He spoke often of key principles in those seemingly far away philosophies and religions *in terms of* our own. This made his writing at the surface familiar and undaunting, which in turn made it more readily accepted—even considered—by our impatient and young society.

The purpose and tone of these early books was but one phase of his career; beginning with *Behold the Spirit*, an extended effort to bridge the chasm between a Christianity of walls, hypocrisy, and spiritual pride, that he perceived as forming before him, and the Christianity that it might had been had it gained awareness of such key precepts from Buddhism and Taoism as non-duality, and the fundamental interrelatedness of the universe-earth-environment relationship.

Seeing life at the most basic level as such a system—as Tao—each event and moment is not fixed as m o m e n t or e v e n t but instead takes on the characteristic of water flowing or birds flying over a still pond—reflected fully and then passed on. This is why water is so commonly the choice metaphor for life among all the Masters throughout the ages and stories (and also fire, which is after all just hot gas flowing up). And one can still observe the contrast between this worldview and the militant morality among modern Evangelicals—often to the exposure of widespread hypocrisy.

Watts wrote these first two books in an attempt to

bridge a gap that he was personally captivated in, and thus mentally stimulated by, between the spiritual beliefs of the East and West.

Tao: the Watercourse Way, which is so purely all in to one side, was the book he was working on when he died in 1971. Juxtaposing this final work with his first two books, you only begin to notice the arc in his development as a person and philosopher. In at least a handful of Watts' books he references those words of 'a Master who said'—

> *"If you walk, just walk. If you sit, just sit, but above all, don't wobble."*

It seems that he learned to live those words well, for he was always sincere and all-there, if nothing else. He did not wobble between what was or what might be, but was fully present in the experiences, thoughts, and opinions of his unique, current state of being. There is a part in the introduction of *Tao: the Watercourse Way*, where Watts' co-author and friend Al Chung-liang Huang (who finished the book after Watts' passing) says this of him:

> *"I noticed a sudden breakthrough in his expression; a look of lightness and glow appeared all around him. Alan had discovered a different way to tell me of his feelings: "Yah...Ha...Ho... Ha! Ho..La Cha Om Ha...Deg deg te te...Ta De De Ta Te Ta...Ha Te Te Ha How...Te Te Te..." ...... Alan knew too that he had never—not in all his books—said it any better than that."*

———

This has been a light, fractured, and incomplete description of Alan Watts the man, as individual, with flaws and passions and a svadharma all his own. We humans are imperfect, so to fashion an unrealistic image of a perfect man is to miss the point, and to endanger the credibility and acceptability of his writing. Looking past his faults is not to ignore them per se, but rather to understand that, in keeping with a fundamental cornerstone of his personal philosophy—*panta rhei*—everything flows.

His transgressions are real—there may be many—however he sought not perfectibility and much less claimed it. An attempt to discredit him for simply being human, subject to emotions, calls for a reminder from *John 8:7*, when Jesus said, "*He that is without sin among you, let him first cast a stone at her.*"

For it is certainly true that whoever should cast judgment is encouraged all the more to look within himself. One defense people use when confronted with this is, "Well, they did worse than me," which is simply moral pride and deflection, to ease their conscience so they can say further, "At least I'm not as bad as them!" When in fact all are equal as sinners, to use that Christian theme, and the measuring of moral compromises depends on the individual, and is thus not an ultimate judgment. "Their sins are worse than mine," is purely opinion and not empirical fact.

Returning to my question of how to reconcile my urge to write with my anxiety of being Watts' tag-along might make a little more sense, for it is seen now that there is the man, his work, and his influence—a unified pattern known as Alan Watts. However each aspect remains individual in their affection[1] on the world—a trinity of sorts.

What I usually ask myself then, is: tagging along to what? For Watts absolutely used his own individual choice of words, and books of reference, titles of projects, and all the other details to express certain ideas, but underlying the details is an experience, and a reality unowned and unown*able*. So on the other hand, here I find my own self. I seem to have had An Experience, with all its details—I grew up in a Christian household with virtually no words on the 'Others', attended a Christian private school with a likewise embargo

---

[1]   From the Latin *afficere;* 'to influence'

on difference, and continue to live in a Christian society filled with unchecked judgment, habitual guilt, and double-standard hypocrisy—and now I am compelled, albeit happily, to write about these experiences and observations as they occur.

In the time before I started writing I decided first to read anything that interested me: aliens, technology, science fiction, fantasy, consciousness, mushrooms. This approach eventually led me to the works of certain authors: Terrence McKenna, Rupert Sheldrake, Fritjof Capra, Ralph Abraham, Hermann Hesse, Carl Sagan.

My interest started noticeably piquing down a particular avenue: comparative religion, psychology, and mythology. In this area I have had as major influences too many people and things to name, but for a few: Joseph Campbell, G.K. Chesterton, D.T. Suzuki, Carl Jung, and, Nikos Kazantzakis.

Spanning all these authors and all this reading, I lived in four houses and two states. During this period I had an incalculable amount of micro and macro influences and inspirations in between anything I might find the time to write about here. I have also experimented with LSD and psilocybin mushrooms a number of times. I have decided that there is the possibility, that, without conflating myself, I and any other *might* have the ability to experience similar states of mind as "Alan Watts" (and any other similarly idolized figure, personally or socially).

This may seem blasphemous to some, as if claiming to *literally* be the person you are relating to, is because of a nifty technique that Watts described as "kicking someone upstairs" similar to putting someone on a pedestal. Watts was, at the time, talking about the problem of people using this way of thinking with Jesus Christ, kicking him upstairs, unreachable and unattainable, and yet always the goal of their religious fulfillment—thereby creating an existential anxiety in the form of 'institutionalized guilt.' Mr. Watts has a famous lecture about this, titled rather explosively, *On Being God.*

On Watts

He spoke of Jesus' followers as taking the Incarnation—God made flesh—and expelling that flesh-made-divine in Jesus back to the heavens as a sort of "Boss's son." These followers, he claims, went further with it by explaining away the life and experiences Jesus had as a 'special privilege' from his real father, the Boss; meaning altogether not the same as everyone else's Father—"You see? Ha ha haa." And Jesus' special kind of enlightenment "stops right there."

After a long while explaining this, Watts finally lets us in on our mistake by saying that we are simply "kicking him upstairs..," missing the message for the man, the forest for the trees. At that moment, you hear a woman in the audience exclaim, "Wooow!" Everyone else seemed to agree, because she was immediately followed by clapping, and a cloud of laughter characteristic of someone being 'realized' out of a mental rut.

This kicking upstairs of people we admire is misplaced and damaging—to ourselves most of all! For we are simply limiting their and our own potential—however well intentioned—which is why I cautioned otherwise in the title of my former essay, and why I consistently try to turn attention to his core subject material, with the man as only a joyful, laughing by-product—to be appreciated but not adored, heeded but not pedestalized.

I bring this technique up to remind myself constantly not to 'unattain' Alan Watts by kicking him upstairs as a godfather of the 70's, a genius with words, or a master of logic, or any other concept. He was, after all, a man with flaws and desires, as well as inspiration and love. His legend has been applied by the admiration of others, due to, I suppose, his reputation as the most unrutted philosopher and by the love of his contemporaries—but admiration left unchecked has room enough to turn into idolatry.[2] And kicking someone

---

[2]   This is not to condemn the idolatrous wholesale, though, for it is likely done with good intentions, and I have surely been in such a place not long ago, or might again be in the future. If so, I hope I am likewise afforded patience over judgment.

upstairs is exactly that.

My original title for this, *Keeping Mr. Watts in the Basement*, was so-named as such in an effort to convey my constant, active effort to not idolize the man and mistake his temporal existence with his influence and legend, which linger on for far longer, and thus retain, in their own way, an infinite aspect. I am expressing this effort of mine directly after saying contradictorily that to idolize or to not is perfectly alright, while keeping in mind Lao-tzu's words from the *Tao Te Ching*:

> *"Know the male,*
> *yet keep to the female:*
> *receive the world in your arms.*
> *If you receive the world,*
> *the Tao will never leave you*
> *and you will be like a little child."*

And how similar:

> *"Verily I say unto you, except ye be converted, and become as little children, ye shall not enter into the kingdom of heaven."*

In other words, keep up the effort—always—of checking the idolatry of any thing or person within yourself, while also remaining open to the fact that you are human, and, should you succumb to your desires, you will be okay—okay not to continue doing the thing, but free from the guilt of a past you cannot change, only a Now in which to act differently.

So, in regards to my own weakness at times with the particular example of Alan Watts, I always strive to keep him in the basement. In this way, I find, the influence he has had on me will not control what I do so much as it will become *a part of* the very base from which what I do emanates. Incidentally, Watts' audio archives are kept in a cement garage I like to think of as a basement, thus again, *Keeping Mr. Watts in the Basement*—literally and metaphorically.

If I give off Wattsian tones through my own writing, it is due only to his profound influence on my own individual perception of the world—along with the thousand and one other influences in music, people, friends, hospital visits, and all the rest—and not in fact due to my conscious recycling of his ideas. And herein lies my issue. For Alan Watts was not an idea or an idealist, he was merely a man who experienced his own life with minimal wobbling, and strove to share the same confidence and joy with his fellow man. And it was contagious!

To the extent, then, that I strive to act as such: with minimum wobbling, I might be said to tag-along to Alan Watts. The ideas of which he writes are too large and infinite to be claimed by any one man, and he knew this! Granted, he had his own particular metaphors and anecdotes for any one subject, but the subject itself—metaphysics and journey of self through the East—one cannot own.

He *knew* this, which is the third reason I named the original essay *Keeping Mr. Watts in the Basement*, for he urged that very thing. Indeed he would have, I think, bellowed a thunderous laugh at the thought of how seriously he is taken.

I will end with one more passage from Lao-tzu's *Tao Te Ching*:

> *If you over esteem great men,*
> *people become powerless.*
> *If you overvalue possessions,*
> *people begin to steal.*
>
> *The Master leads*
> *by emptying people's minds*
> *and filling their cores,*
> *by weakening their ambition*

On Watts

and toughening their resolve.
He helps people lose everything
they know, everything they desire,
and creates confusion
in those who think that they know.

On Leisurely
(as mind)

'Leisurely' has become an interesting word and idea to me—an affirmation of sorts that is lived more than merely an adjective to describe You, as a separate being, needing the medicine of leisure to treat a busy life. Leisurely as active life rather than passive description (come to think of it, I would just as easily, and confusingly, say that leisure as mind is an attitude of passive action).

The distinction of leisure as activity comes to mean more when faced with the assumed and twisted meaning of leisurely as a synonym of mere laziness with a particular aimlessness. I see leisure as the basis and prerequisite to "getting things done." To have a leisurely mind is to have a mind not unnecessarily forced or compelled, while still completing your tasks—almost like the ideal judo stance where one is relaxed and neutral in the middle to avoid the need to draw back from a prematurely assumed position. They simply spring out from the middle without delay. The mind at leisure may be at the apex of its capabilities.

For instance, it is hard to force yourself to remember something... where you left your car keys, your second grade teacher's name, or anything else. It is likewise hard to force feelings to come about—like love or fear—and harder still to force inspiration or creativity, even leadership. You either love or you do not, you're either scared or you are not. Why then do we continue to act on the presumption that leisure is counterproductive, when it is in fact the primary state of mind for creation, genuineness and ingenuity.

We are not actually sitting inside our own heads pulling strings on all the decisions that are being made, micro and macro; if we were, we would be in a state of perpetual headache. We are not really *willing* our feelings into play, but faced with a choice to accept or deny them as they might arise. We make for ourselves a lot of grief by denying these feelings. When we do happen to allow ourselves to accept and agree with what comes our way, we tend not to acknowledge the inevitability and constancy of life—regardless of what we *thought* we were wanting or controlling. You may be able to trick yourself—rather shallowly—that you did want what came your way but it isn't literally so.

We have really been 'graced' with this whole experience. We don't own it, and it is quite a fragile thing to assume we control its goings on. One microscopic tear in a particular vein and you could be dead in minutes. I do not say this to invoke despair, as I am at heart an optimist, only that I am reminded all the time of our lack of control over this life. All good things come from a mysterious cloud (of unknowing) behind, so to speak, the curtains of our life's stage.

We are confused pupils, twirling in the middle of a dark room as objects and events of all sorts are thrown at us from every direction. Some land heavily on our heads, and impact us accordingly. Some miss completely, disregarded if not forgotten, and some we catch mid-air—hoping to learn from them. A few of this last sort are the ones that stoke this belief in us that we indeed can affect and/or control what's going on, simply because of our awareness *of* them. This faux awareness ignores the uncertain effects of those things that are harder to identify, and events that we did not consciously 'allow' to affect us.

The control (or lack thereof) that I speak of is not a matter of being helpless or independent, of despair or hope, but is the practical, everyday manifestation of ego—the idea that we have of ourselves, built up over years of catching one out of every dozen adversarial objects thrown our way. We think we have an ego that does the controlling—a second little man or woman up in our heads pulling those strings, analyzing the thoughts and watching the life that the Body experiences, and filtering out what is good and bad—faced with the impossibility of this task we become vulnerable to despair, claiming things like God is dead, or hates us, or becoming utterly pessimistic and assert that it would be cruel to bring children into such a world as we live in. These things are not *ultimately* true, but subjectively felt based on the mind we choose to understand the world with—the ego that we create.

If we compare the practical effects of leisure and rigidity as mind, we are sure to produce two different worlds entirely: a world of rigidity has no 'give', and as such is not adaptable to even minor fluctuations in the surroundings. In the American Revolutionary War, mostly conventional and rigid tactics were used, but the Patriots incorporated a measure of guerrilla warfare, and thus introduced some 'give' to the battlefield that the British, in their rigidity, could not accommodate. Or even simpler: if you stand rigid in high winds, you will no doubt be blown over, but leaning *into* the wind you find an altogether different, unexpected result.

I have been introduced to this new understanding of leisure as attitude of mind by German philosopher Josef Pieper in his book *Leisure: the Basis of Culture*. I meant this chapter to be a tribute to his impact on me, which I'm certain will continue to reverberate for years to come. Like all good writers, he has not so much spoon feed me philosophical answers—he has begun to permeate the foundation of me; because of this his words are now synonymous with the pattern of "I", for I will be carrying those words and their influence for ever.

I had never read Pieper before but his perspective and authority seemed to strike me—not because he is particularly qualified, but because of his ability to lay out all the pieces of the puzzle in a categorical, sensible and digestible way. He doesn't give off the attitude of professor, but rather of a concerned—not to mention optimistic—man, sharing in his attempt to make our home better.

He begins by detailing ways in which society and state have become compounded with the doctrine of labor as *the* ideal, to the point of fetishization.
He asks,

> *"Is there a sphere of human activity, one might even say of human existence, that does not need to be justified by inclusion in a five-year plan and its technical organization?"*

Before you give your answer, the question might be amended to: "Is there *an acceptable* sphere of human activity . . .", and to that the answer is surely no. We scrutinize all ways of spending a life that have fewer demonstrable benefits to society. This is not to say that it is, so-to-speak, *desirable* to *not* attempt at benefiting society—only that the very nature of this request has evolved into an inescapable requirement—a sort of prison. This is merely *forcing* good deeds, rendered empty out of guilt and obedience, rather than allowing humanheartedness and generosity to appear organically. These good things and deeds are not given as we live now as much as they are loaned, and the collateral for the loan is guilt, for if you don't return the favor in kind, then *what was it all for?*

I don't especially think that a mind at leisure would ask that question in the first place, because it's all for *this* obviously. There is no wasting of time because there is felt no rush to get anywhere. Purists will shout, "You need to stand for something, go *some*where! Or you'll just fall for anything!" And I am not arguing otherwise; to say one should not get stuck is not to say 'stay put'.

From Pieper again,

On Leisurely

> *"Leisure [...] appears [to us] something wholly fortuitous and strange, without rhyme or reason, and, morally speaking, unseemly: another word for laziness, idleness, and sloth."*

He continues,

> *"Idleness, in the old sense of the word, so far from being synonymous with leisure, is more nearly the inner prerequisite which renders leisure impossible. [...] Leisure is only possible when a man is at one with himself..."*

By now you understand that leisure, to Pieper at the least, doesn't 'just mean' anything. It is more than an external affectation on the world, and certainly more than medicine or a pick-me-up *in order to* do work better in the future.[1] Leisure utilized to those ends is hardly a leisurely affair, as the 'ends' to which you are working stay steady in the back of your mind as your driving motivation. And you enjoy the leisure time *only* to the extent and measure in which it benefits and improves your working time—one of the many vicious circles we spin for ourselves.

Leisure, it seems then, is an incredibly important attribute for participants of society. Philosophy itself is defined as "the love of wisdom," and is exceedingly stimulated by an attitude of leisure—for who can, by force, be wise or loving? Those who philosophize are thinkers and observers, and to do either properly, you must stand body and mind still, but you cannot *expect* to gain any thing from standing still. Philosophizing is to be still often and only *happen* to notice the goings-on around you with a particularly contemplative attitude as representative of something greater. Along with

---

[1]   *"...the point of leisure is not to be a restorative, a pick-me-up, whether mental or physical; and though it gives new strength, mentally and physically, and spiritually too, that is not the point."* Pieper, *Leisure: the Basis of Culture.*

philosophy, many other activities are nearly only possible while 'in the pocket' of leisure: falling in love, creating art of any kind, being sensitive to a stroke of genius, and even practical things of the body like riding a bike or falling asleep.

There is also, it seems, a communal aspect to leisure, for if that were the prevailing attitude of friendship or courtship, there would be no prickly expectations or assumptions; you are again like the ideal judo practitioner, right in the middle—ready for All Of It. This neutral stance is not a compromise—it is not to say that you accept agreeably all things that come your way, and that you'd like to stay put in the middle for when they come—I remind you it is *active* leisure. A leisurely mind is empowering in the fact that you do not let *things* become inhibitions to the activity of your life, they fold into the process.

You become like those sage martial artists who can be sitting on the ground eating an apple, with three other experienced fighters surrounding him, while he remains barely stirred—not to be mistaken for unprepared. He is in such a state of complete leisure in his moment of silence that he is able to simply eat his apple, sensitive to every taste bud tingling and every accenting noise around him, which in the next moment may include the attack of an adversary, to which he responds with grace. It's just the next thing, after all; nothing scary, only perhaps mysterious.

At the risk of overquoting Pieper, I am reminded of his words again:

> *"Leisure is a form of silence, of that silence which is the prerequisite of the apprehension of reality: only the silent hear and those who do not remain silent do not hear. Silence [...] means more nearly that the soul's power to "answer" to the reality of the world is left undisturbed."*

This might be the selection I cherish above all and which provokes the deepest reflection, for I have been a person of silent observation for some time, and it has served me well. This is not to say that I demand reward from this course of action, but I have reaped it nonetheless, to my profound gratitude. When I got expelled from Faith Bible, I did not fall into a pit of what-ifs—I simply enjoyed my early summer. When I found myself unable to be contented by a high school that had no interest in educating me, I dropped out and continued my life as it was naturally forming. Never once have I looked back on these events, or any others, and regretted their happening. Instead I have been grateful that my answer to these realities has brought me to this pleasant present, and I only hope I maintain this course.

———————

What I really intend with the chapter subtitle: 'as mind', is: 'as mind, and lacking'. I realize that to prescribe leisure as an attitude that one 'ought' to adopt is in vain, for it can only arise organically within oneself—unforced, "as spring comes and the grass grows, of itself." However, I still find myself wanting to showcase the effects that such an increased sensitivity and acceptance of those silent moments—the silence of the mind—can have. Just as a novel simply begins its story, this drive to showcase leisure should not likely *impose* leisure as *the* ideal—lest it become idolized and corrupted, as labor has been. This showcase should consist then of activities and works that nurture and radiate the principles that come with the philosophical meaning of the word: self-sufficient, and genuine—a beneficial requirement both for the institution of the showcase and for the public to which it speaks.

As mentioned, it wouldn't do for there to be any over the top self-consciousness within this effort. People might simply write poetry, paint, or draw a comic; theorize or philosophize. And these primary activities, done in leisure and simply by happenstance, would make up *Leisurely*.

The plans for such a coordinated effort have yet to

solidly materialize. However, in the spirit of leisure, I am not discouraged—simply open. I know the time will come—perhaps at the wrong time one day, and the right time some other day, but it *will* come.

And in the meantime I will enjoy the things about[2] me, hopefully find myself writing another book or two. Maybe go explore a new part of the country with the family I'm forming. Things will operate as they will, and someday what I envision will *become* one of those things. What's more: someday leisure as mind may naturally regain its respected place in the minds of people at large as *activity*—rather than slandered as lazy, and so remaining undesirable and 'lacking' in our lives.

Pieper often quoted Plato and Aristotle, for reference to a time when the meaning of leisure remained true, and this from the latter stuck with me:

> *"A man will live [leisurely], not to the extent that he is a man, but to the extent that a divine principle dwells within him."*

---

2   Used to indicate movement in an area . . .

"I am a sinner who's probably gonna sin again
Lord forgive me, Lord forgive me
Things I don't understand,
Sometimes I need to be alone"

Kendrick Lamar

On My Self
(and its confessions)

I confess
> in this scenario,
> you are the priest
> and I am the sinner.

> So
> if you would
> sit tight and listen:

> I have much to learn
> much to say
> and more to convey
> than I could ever *completely* say.

I confess
> that at times
> I feel incomplete,
> insecure,
> and unoriginal.

> Sometimes that's okay.
> They become the days of My Self
> and not Your Self.
> In these days I find

On My Self

my defensiveness—
still more importantly
my pensiveness.

I confess

that I relish in this confessional;
of breaking the fourth wall
which has apparently lingered
strong
since two thousand and five, on.

I've barely had the wherewithal
these past thirteen years gone
of the complicated source
from which my blessings have shone.

I confess

that I might want to have it all.
Too much.
To be received well,
two rare bookshelves,
and an empty mind unswelled.

I'd like to write my books,
I'd like two dogs in their nooks.

I'd like my love Ísa
to look right up at me
just cause.

I confess

I might just want what you do too:
patience from these strangers,
love from significant others,
no judgment from like-sinners;
awareness of my faults
and

On My Self

knowledge of my strengths.

I confess

this is me, Jacob George Roloff.

I confess

I enjoy this experiment
of running my own life.
Here I am, or there I go.
I can tell you my true thoughts,
or feel like laying low—
aloof—
watching over the world
to resist getting caught awhirl.

I'll likely not like this piece
when this piece of me has gone—
passed on—
when a new thing
inspires
a new piece,
when I feel myself aloof up there again!

It's peaceful up there;
it's clear and quite sterile.
There's beauty in it, to be sure.
However
truthfully, I might be scared of those heights.
I can't keep myself still
from wondering how it goes below.

I confess

sometimes I just want to play a game—
the game—
until I've quite had my fill.

I always think of the folks who don't know me,

On My Self

the ones who
by nature of our relationship
do not affect their judgment upon me.
I can act a fool or a wise
and it would be taken as simply as it comes.
These types allow me a certain special freedom
that I just can't find in the fine folks of formality or
friendship.
This is to be nothing *against* anyone
and everything *for* everyone.
I mean no harm completely to any that might feel it, and
incidentally reiterate all delayed appreciation
for those who need to hear it.

I confess

I have lost my track completely,
gotten caught up in some swirl once again
of thoughts, opinions, fears,
of what I want to tell the world again

while showing you My Self—
my rambling mind, my desire for love
my resisting this world
and
my hypocrisy in longing for it . . .

I confess

to you
timeless reader:
I don't want to be so different.

I've just decided to accept my self,
seeing that there is no other way.

And on that note I should say

On My Self

I confess
 here as well,
 I want truly to change the world.

 First, by changing my own
 second, by understanding yours
 and then
 by meeting once more in the middle,
 rapt in maya—
 —joined in worship of 'All Of It.'

On the State
(and of spirit)

I keep seeing people ask how we got where we are; it seems all dreary in the news, but I can't stop thinking of the *universal* truth that for every action there is an equal and opposite *re*action. I do not agree with or approve of any one thing that our current government administration has done, but I don't see it as an end in any way. I think it is more sensible to see these unfavorable decisions as formative material for greatness in Generation Next. This isn't empty optimism but bona fide truth. Resistance and hardship are primers to strengthen character—be it cruelly or not—and such widespread corruption as we are witnessing is going to touch and motivate an enormous amount of young people in a revolutionary way. This daily dreadful feeling is not the end we are fighting, but a moment in the eye of a new world building; a moment of *bifurcation* in our time, where our actions are more immediately realized in their effects on the future. In other words, the stars (literally, too) are aligning in many ways, indicating a tipping point of sorts that must in relatively quick time, go one way or the other.[1]

---

[1]   This thought has two possible ends: it goes the good way or the bad way. To us raised in familiarity with the certain duality of Heaven and Hell, of God and Satan, it takes only the slightest emotional, psychological trigger to compel us feeling despair, thinking it *must* be bad if its not good—*and thats it!* We separate our foods, and our Gods, and don't allow them to even mentally interact, whereas in the most common symbol of

On the State

The political situation of our time is more complex than ever. AS always there are humans involved, bringing with them their emotions of stubbornness, fear, and confusion. These emotions are then manifested in several ways in duality-politics: bigotry and nationalism, isolation, refusing those in need. It seems we have allowed the common denominator for what it means to be human to be swept out from under us.

We killed God, and with cold sweats clung to the world. We created a reality of our own, below Him, yet deeply *for* Him, of things and civilization and the magic of technology, and pedestalized ourselves as above the usable, vulnerable, powerless world. In effect, we have built ourselves into a sort of limbo set firmly between celebration of our (quite mysteriously) given life, of God and of his created, and our ability to extrapolate and *use* the Other created elements, transforming them into our present mode of society and acceptable discourse.

Anything religious and mystical is now considered 'scientifically' as supernatural, which is to say fantastical; and a life by science is to the religious instantly decried as being part of innumerable agendas, or blatant blasphemy. Of course there are dozens of denominations for any religion and so these criteria, on a communal scale, are positively indecipherable.

Speaking of religion and of God, I personally mean an 'internal life' for lack of better, less confusing language, and perhaps knowledge of the larger life within us, which is in fact of the same nature *as* God—as we are 'masks of Shiva.' And speaking of this inner life, I suppose I mean spirit. Our spirit, in a healthy state, is what affords us quite random, however

---

the East, the *taijitu,* the exact opposite sentiment is expressed: in that these opposites are as much dependent and *one of* one another as they might be opposed. Contemplating this relationship is key to understanding failure, and growth; so, whichever way it goes, it goes. One should act just such a way that befits and accommodates each individual situation. Always strive for the good, obviously, but accept the bad as *of one process with* the good; in this way, atrocities and injustices toward yourself and the world are not *literally* an end in themselves—the question is the effort, as well as you are able, to make it as it should be—to *balance.*

common, bursts of inspiration to be human in our most basic and pure ways. To do a thing without cause or meaning aside from itself is to have quite a complete experience, not twisted and cut off as You that is Doing the Thing, but, the thing 'thinging', and you 'youing.'

The base from which the most human of human attitudes springs, is the spirit. For the health of our spirit, it simply won't do to have this life be *for* "just blackness" at the end, or any other so depressing a tale as suffering for*ever*. Working with the symbolic meaning of the *taijitu,* it would benefit us to apply it to this body/spirit dichotomy. Doing so we would see that we are just now our bodies, although we are ultimately more than our bodies. We are dealing with two realities, two points of view here and neither necesssarily conquers the other. They exist not merely in coexistence but symbiosis. The two realities would be those defined as either *for* this world only or for something truer and more eternal. The two points of view that contrast here are that of universality and of ego.

Our ego is the very useful and handy image that we structure around our true selves (spirit) in order to communicate in such a vast and, only very recently, interconnected world. The so-called universal point of view is that which accepts both body and mind while not exclusively choosing them, and accepts also the spirit while not choosing *it.* The universal point of view creates something altogether new in point of view and experience—the experience fades with the moment but the doorway to that point of view can never be closed and so lingers right behind the eyes. Seeing something with a glimpse of such a point of view, you might realize as the astronauts did when looking back on our pale blue dot, ~~that~~ we realize that we are relative to a much larger process of spectacular magnitude. This point of view realizes everything in its proper place: as unexpendable energy and thus not especially bothered at the prospect of death (*in that moment*[2])

---

[2]   To have this universal point of view is not to keep it but to experience it. To truly have it, you must let it continue its process and leave your mind; it will influence you in the most fundamental of ways by

for any one of life's subjects, for it is not 'dying' or 'being removed,' but returning to its purer essence.

This enduring contest between points of view forces the objection that this is some sort of fatalism, but as being a Trinity suggests: one thing is not the whole thing. You are not, in other words, supposed to realize this thing and give up on life. No, it matters all the more and requires your participation by nature of your existence at all. You *are* this matter, this maya. This belief though, of our 'end' and meaning, the definition to our lives, I don't find as common among my peers. Because of this, I'd say for almost certain that what we're dealing with above all in our present day is a sickness, or at the very least ignorance, of spirit.

This language, 'sickness of spirit,' is instantly received and understood as being the condescension of the morally prideful if not tyrannical. Unfortunately I am not sure that there could be anything executively done to change this attitude, but it is certainly not *necessarily* true; and by nature of it not being necessarily so, we are afforded at least the *possibility* of this prognosis being accurate to some degree. If this were to be true in any respect, the 'afflicted' would be operating with and promulgating this tilt in the balance of spirit into the world and into their politics. Over time there would become whole areas of society evolving with and institutionalizing this affliction, as well as being governed by it.

The word myopia means literally closing the eyes, from the Greek *myein* "to shut" + *ops* "eye, sight" and forcing a bit of wordplay here, utopia means literally 'nowhere' from the Greek *ou* "not" + *topos* "place".[3] Myopia is primarily a <u>medical term for optical short-sightedness, but can be used</u> nature of its *feeling* (as opposed to feeling*s*). You must in other words have nearly as much 'unenlightenment' as you would enlightenment; as much time playing your part in the world as you spend watching from backstage.

[3]   It has since been redefined, originally appearing as the title of the book *Utopia* (1516) about an imaginary island with ideal social structure. Our modern misunderstanding of it is actually quite a funny joke, for we present it as the definition of an *ideal world*, with its true root meaning essentially "*not here*."

philosophically or politically to imply a lack of perspective or tunnel vision.

Now, rather than assuming the Greek *ops*, we might substitute *topos* after *myein* in order to create a word meaning "shut place". Used philosophically this wouldn't mean the imaginary paradise or hell for we have created, and are creating, the all too real myopia (*myein-topos*) in front of us in the form of bigotry, nationalism, *literal* walled and shut off borders. Furthermore we are, as a people, becoming less and less concerned and involved with one another and the integrity of our individual and collective Spirit—our very basic wellness.

The Spirit—that from which all genuine life, action, feeling, *politics*, and sensitivity springs—would then of course be the central mover to our affection on the world. In that case, the integrity of such a foundation should be of sure importance, if not at least interest. This integrity is maintained only through acceptance of those things through which the Spirit is expressed, by which of course I mean creation in its myriad of form, and of the Spirit itself.

I have mentally scribbled down a few possible points of departure toward this sort of foundation-maintenance, which are not meant to be prescriptions or prophecy, but a supplemental addition to an ongoing conversation. I'm assuming that I have the authority to join in this conversation by the simple fact of my experiencing life as an expression of this same Spirit as yourself—*of one nature.*

My first thought, by no means a new revelation and rather a reiteration and combination of the philosophies of Watts and Pieper, is to address our lingering obsession with work-as-purpose, and specifically always needing to suffer and toil to attain those things of true value. This leads people to think terrible things about success and of those who do not subscribe to the same criteria. This would lead one, while looking at a gallery of art, to ask the somewhat meaningless question of, "How long did it take? For in the respectable world of work, the *correct* answer is that it took a terribly long time, and that you poured over your thoughts for months in order to get the inspiration required. Only *then* is it acceptable, worthy, and good art, for look at the work you put in!

I do not believe our purpose could possibly be to simply toil (for these days even our leisure time is infected with this work-bug, and is used only to *do work better, later*). An acknowledgment of this very fundamental attitude we have would be a first step in tempering it, and not allowing it to so dominate every sphere of life.

Speaking literally of work, there is no issue—no issue in *doing* things.[4] The issue is on another dimension of the word—of the inescapability of our requirement that what we do *must* serve as a utility and beneficiary to society, or must at least serve progress along a very defined line. As we have grown it, the attitude toward the liberal arts of writing, painting, poetry, and philosophizing is one of disdain, if not altogether felt as irrelevant and *use*less.

> *"..the proletarian is the man who is fettered to the process of work. ... To be fettered to work means to be bound to this vast utilitarian process.."*[5]

The dilemma as far as this so-called obsession with work goes, is to become unfettered to solely utilitarian purposes for our work, which brings to mind the quote from Thoreau: "It is not enough to be busy. So are the ants. The question is: What are we busy about?"

Pieper coined this acknowledgment and temperament, "deproletarianizing". The reason we find ourselves here, he

---

[4]   The glaringly obvious in this discussion is that I have personally been afforded a great advantage economically as I have been 'employed' since I was seven-years-old in a very lucrative industry. It is an advantage that I recognize is responsible for giving me this particular perspective on our leisure/work dichotomy. Those very many who are working for survival or family, *in extremis,* can hardly be expected to waste the time revolutionizing their mere *perception* of work, when there is real work that needs to be done. Both points of view remain valid and *real,* however, and although my unique economic situation has made it a non-necessity to retain a longterm conventional job, I am not averse to its value or benefit.

[5]   *Leisure: the Basis of Culture* by Josef Pieper *(1948)*

argues, is that the end meaning of our life has been hijacked by an amorphous 'other' to serve its own purposes and ends, and being so amorphous, our solution is best approached in several ways. Deproletarianizing would thus mean:

> "..enlarging the scope of life beyond the confines of merely useful servile work, and widening the sphere of servile work to the advantage of the liberal arts; and this process, once again, can only be carried out by combining three things: by **giving the wage-earner the opportunity to save and acquire property**, by **limiting the power of the state**, and by **overcoming inner impoverishment of individual**."[6]

This goal would be no simple one, and so demands plenty of devoted time, for even after completion it would require constant upkeep; yet still, the acknowledgment of this even *being* a goal, having a secure and Spirit-accepting end, has yet to be felt on a large scale. It is nonetheless one of many different avenues to pursue on the road to improving the health and integrity of self and spirit.

This brings us to my second thought, which is our collective trend toward denial of any sort of higher power. We've promised ourselves to a cold world of facts and things, which are simply measurements representing the real thing, never *reaching* the real thing, but instead forcing only the discovery of smaller and smaller measurements *ad infinitum*. Speaking dramatically, we have forsaken our perfect[7] nature in lieu of imitations of natural rhythms and patterns, built in reverence to nothing but progress. We have been cut off, or rather have cut ourselves off, from our divine source.

From Jung in his *Memories, Dreams, Reflections*:

---

[6]   Ibid. [bold my own]

[7]   From the Latin *per*- "through, completely" + *facere* "do"; *perfectus* "completed"—our "complete" life in knowledge of our divine nature.

On the State

> *"Life has always seemed to me like a plant that lives on its rhizome. Its true life is invisible, hidden in the rhizome. The part that appears above ground lasts only a single summer. Then it withers away—an ephemeral apparition. ... Yet I have never lost a sense of something that lives and endures underneath the eternal flux. What we see is the blossom, which passes. The rhizome remains."*

All life as we know it is in fact the blossoming of this rhizome, and that is certainly beautiful language for describing our predicament of existence.

Still, we are left with the practical issues between Science and Religion, eyes and faith, body and mind. These problems are indeed only of our world and not indicative of the nature of the Spirit, albeit an expression of it. For the Spirit ought not and can not be confined to either side of our worldly dilemmas; it retains both.

Of our practical dilemma regarding the big ones—Science and Religion—I keep falling back to the thought of our worldly population, with the big 10^{10} (10,000,000,000) seeming imminent—a milestone of numerical and evolutionary significance. Regardless of those, it is simply a lot of people. All the more so when compared to the estimated population of the world when the prophets of religion were walking, or when modern science was beginning to be practiced. Which is to say that the requirements for symbiosis between these two ideologies, not to mention their adherents, are a great deal more complex, and so the solutions of the past in and of themselves will be inadequate and unsatisfying to the needs of our present.

As I have mentioned, it seems likely to me that we are indeed inside an evolutionary moment of bifurcation in which our actions are more meaningful and immediate in their results. That being so, it bears discussing the choices we are making as a society, what we are building and promulgating. Obviously, we cannot executively dictate these societal changes, but a society is indeed made up of individuals, and so in these moments of bifurcation, individuals are ~~as well~~ more likely to be impacted by the conversations, feelings, and experiences of their lives than before. Every day, we make choices privately and publicly that *will* impact the direction of our time to come. We can effectively, in this period of time, look straight at our own evolution, reflect on it, and then consciously urge it in one direction or another.

Therefore, we have now the perfect opportunity for growth through a shedding of our myopia and absolutism, lacking in recognition of that 'divine rhizome'. In the place of this aged mind and perception we would, without compromising its essence, use these past ways of understanding life to form something wholly different and 'higher' in incorporation.

It would not do for this new way of thinking to be too evidently related to an old tradition, for it would too quickly lose its credibility as a rehashing of the same-old. Neither can it be any 'new age' creation of superficiality, with no tradition upon which it is founded, and so also immediately seen as unfit and uninspiring. This new end and "New Mind" we are in the midst of deciding upon *must* therefore be born from the lessons, death, and ashes, of our "Past Mind". This conscious effort toward realignment of our personal, as well as societal, end and purpose is indeed the most fundamental aspect to the health of our Spirit, and is thus of utmost importance and primary attention—that is, what attitudes and reverberations we are personally and politically bringing to fruition.

Another suggested approach to our problem and available in every situation, is to let things operate as they will. This is indeed a very hard position for our present minds to understand, much less adopt, not only due to our insistence of the immutability of duality, but also in our alarming lack of faculty for faith and knowing when to trust it. We might assume, although I am not saying, that our letting things happen would mean to sit and do nothing *for ever* until directed otherwise, but this course of action is rather more course than action; more attitude, less *direct*ion. And so what does it being an attitude actually mean?

When it is said to 'let things be', the words end just back there, and so our present understanding, too easily convinced of and satisfied with our description *of* the world, forgets to consider that we may not have the full view of this; and takes it as a one-dimensional direction. This is a danger all too commonly realized, for 'where the line is drawn'—be it national lines or moral, materialistic or religious lines— has been the root issue for war throughout history, and the problem is the same here.

Christian Scientists believe that their congregation should not accept modern medical help or medicine[8] and should rather attempt to pray ailments away. They base this on various passages from the Bible in which people were healed by miracles. There is anecdotal testimony to the effectiveness of this and I don't necessarily doubt it, but that's certainly not where I am drawing *my* line. The common refutation to this belief (which I share) is posing the question, "How do you know that God has not placed these innovators of medicine on earth, throughout time, for the specific reason of carrying out these miracles in healing?"

This same sort of argument is posed to the pacifistic attitude of letting things be, and it's hard to argue! The question is relevant: When *do* you do something? Sure, you let it happen, but then what?[9] And I might suppose that this is impossible to define for another person. As the adage goes: "I only know it when I see it."

So what *are* the two sides of this line, this scenario

---

[8]   There are a few, quite modern, acceptable situations to see a doctor, however this is generally their belief.

[9]   Perhaps pacifistic should be substituted with passivism (n) -- the quality of being passive. However, passive in our modern vernacular means, like leisure, something closer to lazy; whereas the Chinese have a different concept of this attitude in *wu wei* (pronounced WOO-WAY) Translated literally it means "non doing". But used in their way, it means something closer to "going with the flow" or "way of least resistance"; it means to be wise with your energy, harnessing the already moving process of life in order to incorporate your own goings-on with*in* it. It might be described contradictorily as doing-non-doing.

of you watching and a thing happening? It could be called an issue of sensitivity, to your feelings, and knowings. The decision to get involved or to let things be is already made, and your part in the process is to be sensitive enough to respond accordingly. Simply *is it the moment* in which you are to get involved—or isn't it? It answers itself. The problem is in our suppression of this sensitivity through over-stimulation (that hardly needs to be identified, the issue is so intertwined with the way we live). It seems, in order to gain the capability to rationalize this way of *wu wei* (definition), and to be sensitive to its uses, we would have to radically change the way we take care of our mind.

Our vision of our brain seems to be of utility, and our mind of ego. We seem to reduce the definition of our thoughts, feelings, aspirations, and associations to our name, and see our brain as a computer we happen to have gotten for free—or rather on loan. What we need to realize is that these things that we implicitly see as controlled, or wrangled at the least by us, are in fact of the same nature and *on the same level* as this observer making all these conclusions. You've got the power, and you're all of it, so be it![10]

With an inkling of sensitivity, a new, inspiring life's end giving renewed and infinite purpose, and self-awareness of our state of affairs in the first place, I'm less wondering how we got here than I am excited for the improvement and growth ahead of us as a species.

I think we should all be more optimistic than the events at present let on. The leadership coming from young people around the world is inspiring but also this change in general mind toward *caring,* for other people and the world around us is prevalent. As I have mentioned earlier, the apparent metaphor is that a swell is occurring; the lack of leadership and representation from older generations is receding—too slowly for my taste—in disgrace, and replacing it is the spirituous and revolutionary, with a distinctly less myopic perspective.

This trend is showing no sign of slowing, and every

---

[10]   Amen!

indication of growing. The March For Our Lives movement, birthed after the eighteenth mass shooting of 2018, in a well-received but long overdue effort to break the National Rifle Association's choke-hold on Congressional representatives—all led by the very students who have been so misrepresented and endangered, and who have had enough, and plan on changing things. The social consensus on the issue of gun control was—*essentially*—to let bureaucracy fail. These students have clearly drawn the line and galvanized the people's support to legitimately turn the tide—for their lives.

There's plenty more of the same leadership and courage in the generation to come.. These voices should not be, and indeed will not be, shut down or silenced. "How did we get here?"—no, we shouldn't be thinking that just yet. We should be putting our faith and support in the ones who are raising their voices and actually *daring* to change the world in which they live. Our state of politics and of mind is henceforth overdue for a rehaul, and a little more deliberate and caring attention.

I am wholeheartedly optimistic for our future and our future leaders, and in support of the crazy ones, per Steve Jobs, who are empowered enough to think that they can change the world. Those who stock their minds well are never bored with themselves and their imagination, neither the world—which is of the utmost stimulation to a curious mind.

From the late Stephen Hawking:

> *"Remember to look up at the stars and not down at your feet. Try to make sense of what you see and wonder about what makes the universe exist. Be curious."*

On the State

Afterword

I have in mind two quotes, here at the end, from two vastly different people with vastly different birthplaces, backgrounds, interests, careers, struggles, and impact on society.

The first is from the preface of Alan Watts' *The Supreme Identity*:

> *"I am not one who believes that it is any necessary virtue in the philosopher to spend his life defending a consistent position. It is surely a kind of spiritual pride to refrain from 'thinking out loud,' and to be unwilling to let a thesis appear in print until you are prepared to champion it to the death. .. for a man cannot think rightly alone, and the philosopher must publish his thought as much to learn from criticism as to contribute to the sum of wisdom. If, then, I sometimes make statements in an authoritative and dogmatic manner, it is for the sake of clarity rather than from the desire to pose as an oracle."*

This it is largely my purpose with this book—to think rightly in a way that satisfies my need to express and that also contributes to a larger conversation. I once indeed thought that I had to champion my opinions to the bitter end, but I've since learned how to yield, both in dealing with criticism and with my own vision of myself actually stating these opinions.

Afterword

I am simply participating in the process of growth and in no way presume to have the final word. I am opening myself to conversation and will not accept condemnation simply for thinking out loud.

The second quote, stuck in my mind in tandem with the first, is from Kendrick Lamar and his 2011 album *Section.80* from the song *Ab-Souls Outro (feat. Ab-Soul)*:

> *"Some of ya'll wonder how I can talk about money, hoes, clothes, God, and history all in the same sentence. You know what all those things have in common? Only half of the truth, when you tell it. .. I'm not on the outside lookin' in, I'm not on the inside lookin' out, I'm in the dead fuckin' center, lookin' around. .. So the next time I talk about money, hoes, clothes, God, and history all in the same sentence, just know I meant it, and you felt it, cause you too are searching for answers.."*

It is evident to me that these two seemingly disparate generational philosophers have conjured the same sentiment of foundational curiosity, tolerance, and respect; a sentiment that I hope to have been afforded and received with the reading of this book.

Throughout the writing of this, I have been immensely impacted by music—as much as, if not more, than the degree to which my favored books have impacted me. The music of my fiancée's late brother Tomás has inspired me no less than the globally famous names I have mentioned throughout. The song of his from which I have borrowed the title for this book has moved me especially.

The stories of his life are almost unbelievable, and his passion for living life equally so.

His humanheartedness seems unmatched, something I know only from reputation; for when he was sixteen he had open heart surgery to correct a hole in his heart "the size of a golf ball." He was told he would not live past his twenties, and he unfortunately did not. This was due, however, to his passion and love for life, and in defiance of the inadequacies of his anatomy. He was a traveler of epic proportions, relative to the drab lives that most of us in the everyday world live.

He traveled to nearly as many countries as years lived on this earth—mostly by foot, scarcely by car, sometimes by freight train, and occasionally by veggie-oil-powered bus. If he had lived in the 1960s he would've surely been called a Beatnik, but these days people like him go by terms such as Dirty Kids or Oogles. The stories from his travels, which I hear secondhand from his older brother Nicolás, his father Tomás, his little sister Izzy, and the countless others that he impacted in life, and death, are too numerous to be repeated.

One of my favorites is recorded in one of his journals, which are almost prophetic in their content. He had taken a vow of silence for a time, speaking and communicating to no one in reaction to his deep insecurity of taking up too much space, physically and energetically, in a group of people.

Tomás was a physically big man, roughly 6'5" and 300lbs and his personality was similarly proportioned in its magnetism and seemed to demand people's attention. He didn't *always* love that. During this spell of silence, he was in Mexico and walking down a market street when he saw a man wearing a shirt that he rather liked. He was street fluent in Spanish, but it didn't matter—the two men didn't need words, and with a few hand motions, disregarding all supposed barriers of culture and language—even silence—they exchanged shirts and went on their way.

Although I never met Tomás, I respect and even love him still. His music and journals are the only ways I can 'see' him, and so I keep a copy of his solo album *Bear Feat* in my car at all times. *Out To See* struck me in particular with its lyrics. I fear however that their meaning can only be accurately felt through hearing his experienced, raspy yet kind voice singing them. I am luckier for this experience, to be certain, and I surely would not have written this book were it not for this man I never met.

Life is funny in that way. I can hear his giggle from track 04 now...

Long live Toe!

Jacob G. Roloff
May 2018

"Out To See"
by Tomás (Toe) Garretón

I was sittin' under a palm tree when a coconut hit my head /
I woke up in the morning an' I found myself dead /
I stared into my own eyes, it gave me such a start /
I reached into my chest and I pulled out my own heart /
I built a raft of skin n' bones, and cooked the rest of me /
Raised no flags, said no goodbyes, I headed out to sea /

I'm goin' away /
I'm going out to see /

(ohhh ohhh ohh oh)

I've left this world behind /
I'm goin' out to see /

(ohhh ohhh ohh)

I'll never be back alive, /
I'm goin' out to see

(x2)

¡Larga vida Toe!

Jacob Roloff is an Oregon native who loves biking, traveling, 35mm film photography, and writing. Reading was a great joy growing up and he immersed himself in the works of Terrence Mckenna, Alan Watts, and Hermann Hesse. In 2017, he published a short work titled *Verbing*. *Out To See* is a more in-depth perspective on some of the same subjects and themes explored in *Verbing*.

He currently lives in Helvetia, Oregon, with his fiancée Isabel and their two dogs, Moose and Luna.

© Isabel Rock

Made in the USA
Monee, IL
10 December 2019

18304868R00085